MICROWAVE I

Microwave Notes:

Understanding how your microwave works is easy — just think of it as a chain reaction. As microwaves penetrate the food, they cause the food molecules to vibrate. This in turn causes heat which cooks the food; the cooking process spreads from the outside towards the center.

Because food cooks from the outside in, there are some techniques you should use to avoid uneven cooking:

— position the thickest portion of irregularly shaped food toward the walls of the microwave where it will receive more microwave energy.

— when stirring foods, move the food from the outside of the dish towards the center and vice-versa.

— rotating is a technique used with such foods as cakes or puddings which cannot be stirred. If a recipe calls for this procedure, simply rotate the dish a quarter or half turn (depending on the size of the mold).

You can cover food with the matching casserole top or in some cases with sheets of paper towel, plastic wrap or waxed paper. When you use plastic wrap be sure to pierce the wrap or tuck up one corner to allow excess steam an escape.

Although it is not essential to have a cupboard stacked with special microwave utensils, it is advisable to invest in at least several casserole dishes, plus perhaps a serving platter and a rectangular glass dish. Some dessert recipes call for particular cake molds; refer to the recipe for a description.

Because microwave ovens vary in terms of maximum power and power settings, you should study the following chart before you begin any recipes. Our test microwave was 650 watts.

Setting	Approximate wattage	Percent of power
HIGH	650	100
MEDIUM-HIGH	485	75
MEDIUM	325	50
LOW	160	25

Please consult your manufacturer's guide booklet if you are not already familiar with your microwave's controls and settings.

Mozza Sticks

(serves 2)

1 SERVING	352 CALORIES	17g CARBOHYDRATE
30g PROTEIN	22g FAT	0.5g FIBER

Setting: HIGH
Cooking Time: 14 minutes
Utensil: Roasting Rack
8 cups (2 L) casserole with cover

8	slices bacon
8	2 in (5 cm) carrot sticks
8	2 in (5 cm) mozzarella sticks
	salt and pepper

Arrange bacon on roasting rack; microwave 7 minutes. Cover with paper towel to prevent spattering.

Remove bacon from rack and set aside. Clean rack for later use.

Place carrot sticks in casserole; pour in about 1 cup (250 ml) water. Cover and microwave 6 minutes.

Drain carrots and rinse under cold water for several seconds.

Team carrot sticks with cheese sticks; carefully wrap with bacon. Secure with toothpicks.

Place bundles on roasting rack and season generously. Microwave 1 minute uncovered.

Snacking Eggs

(serves 4)

1 SERVING	594 CALORIES	20g CARBOHYDRATE
34g PROTEIN	42g FAT	trace FIBER

Setting: HIGH
Cooking Time: 6½ minutes
Utensil: 8 cups (2 L) casserole with cover

1 tbsp	(15 ml) butter
1	onion, diced
1	garlic clove, smashed and chopped
1	green pepper, diced
¾ lb	(375 g) piece Italian sausage, sliced
4	large eggs, beaten
1 cup	(250 ml) cubed mozzarella
4	large hot buns
	salt and pepper

Place butter, onion, garlic and green pepper in casserole. Cover and microwave 2 minutes.

Add sausage slices and microwave 1 minute covered.

Pour in beaten eggs and season well; mix with wooden spoon. Microwave 1½ minutes uncovered.

Stir eggs well and add cheese. Microwave 1 minute uncovered. Stir again; microwave 1 minute uncovered.

Serve on hot buns.

Stuffed Mushrooms

(serves 4)

1 SERVING	211 CALORIES	5g CARBOHYDRATE
5g PROTEIN	15g FAT	1.0g FIBER

Setting: MEDIUM

Cooking Time: 3 minutes

Utensil: Stoneware serving platter

1	bunch fresh watercress
3 tbsp	(45 ml) walnuts
1	tomato, cut in chunks
1	garlic clove, smashed and chopped
¼ cup	(50 ml) olive oil
4 tbsp	(60 ml) grated Parmesan cheese
16	large mushroom caps
	few drops Tabasco sauce
	few drops Worcestershire sauce
	salt and pepper

Wash watercress well and dry. Place in food processor and blend until almost puréed.

Add walnuts and tomato; blend until puréed.

Add garlic and oil; blend several seconds. Add cheese, Tabasco, Worcestershire, salt and pepper; blend again for several seconds.

Stuff mushroom caps with mixture and arrange on stoneware plate. Microwave 3 minutes.

Serve as an appetizer.

Place washed dried watercress in bowl of food processor. Blend until almost puréed.

 After oil and garlic have been incorporated, add cheese and remaining ingredients; blend for several seconds.

Add walnuts and tomato; blend until puréed.

 Stuff mushroom caps with mixture. Microwave 3 minutes

Artichoke Appetizer

(serves 4)

1 SERVING	166 CALORIES	13g CARBOHYDRATE
9g PROTEIN	10g FAT	1.0g FIBER

Setting: HIGH and MEDIUM-HIGH

Cooking Time: 5 minutes

Utensil: 8 cups (2 L) casserole with cover
Stoneware serving platter

14 oz	(398 ml) can artichoke bottoms, drained and rinsed
2 tbsp	(30 ml) butter
½ lb	(250 g) mushrooms, sliced
½	celery stalk, very finely chopped
1	small onion, finely chopped
2	slices crisp bacon, chopped
1	garlic clove, smashed and chopped
3 tbsp	(45 ml) ricotta cheese
	salt and pepper

Arrange artichoke bottoms on stoneware platter; set aside.

Place butter, mushrooms, celery and onion in casserole. Cover and microwave 3 minutes at HIGH.

Mix in bacon, garlic and cheese; season well.

Fill artichoke bottoms with mixture. Microwave 2 minutes at MEDIUM-HIGH uncovered.

Sausage Sloppy Joes

(serves 4)

1 SERVING	376 CALORIES	35g CARBOHYDRATE
16g PROTEIN	21g FAT	2.0g FIBER

Setting: HIGH

Cooking Time: 10 minutes

Utensil: 12 cups (2.8 L) casserole with cover

1 tbsp	(15 ml) butter
1	onion, sliced
1	green pepper, thinly sliced
28 oz	(796 ml) can tomatoes, drained and chopped
½ cup	(125 ml) stuffed green olives, chopped
2	small pepperoni sausages, sliced
1 tbsp	(15 ml) cornstarch
2 tbsp	(30 ml) cold water
4	hamburger buns, toasted open
1¼ cups	(300 ml) grated mozzarella cheese
	salt and pepper

Place butter, onion and green pepper in casserole. Cover and microwave 5 minutes.

Stir in tomatoes and season to taste. Add olives and pepperoni; microwave 4 minutes covered.

Mix cornstarch with water; stir into casserole and microwave 1 minute uncovered.

Separate hamburger buns and place tops over bottoms. Set on cookie sheet and spoon sausage mixture over bread. Top with cheese and broil in conventional oven until melted.

Serve immediately.

Meatloaf Muffins

(serves 4)

1 SERVING	293 CALORIES	55g CARBOHYDRATE
41g PROTEIN	6g FAT	1.0g FIBER

Setting: HIGH

Cooking Time: 5 minutes

Utensil: Muffin Ring

2	small potatoes, peeled and grated fine
2	carrots, pared and grated
1 lb	(500 g) lean ground beef
1	egg
2	medium onions, chopped and cooked
¼ tsp	(1 ml) allspice
½ tsp	(2 ml) chili powder
	salt and pepper

Combine potatoes and carrots in large bowl. Add beef and mix together well.

Add remaining ingredients and mix until thoroughly incorporated.

Press mixture into cups of muffin ring. Microwave 5 minutes uncovered.

Remove and let cool slightly before serving. These are ideal for after-school snacks and are handy to have on weekends.

Combine potatoes and carrots in large bowl.

Add beef and mix together well.

Add egg and remaining ingredients and mix until thoroughly incorporated.

Press mixture into cups of muffin ring.

Shrimp on Muffins

(serves 4)

1 SERVING	472 CALORIES	40g CARBOHYDRATE
23g PROTEIN	23g FAT	1.0g FIBER

Setting: HIGH

Cooking Time: 8 minutes

Utensil: 12 cups (2.8 L) casserole with cover

3 tbsp	(45 ml) butter
1 lb	(500 g) mushrooms, diced
1	shallot, chopped
4 tbsp	(60 ml) flour
1½ cups	(375 ml) hot milk
4 oz	(113 g) can shrimp, drained and rinsed
¼ tsp	(1 ml) nutmeg
4	English muffins, lightly toasted whole
1 cup	(250 ml) grated cheddar cheese
	salt and pepper

Place butter, mushrooms and shallot in casserole. Cover and microwave 4 minutes.

Mix in flour. Pour in milk and season; mix again. Microwave 4 minutes uncovered.

Add shrimp and nutmeg; mix well.

Using small knife pare away some of bread in the middle of each muffin. Place on cookie sheet and fill holes with shrimp mixture. Top with grated cheese and broil in conventional oven until melted.

Serve as a light lunch.

Bacon Bite

(serves 4)

1 SERVING	131 CALORIES	7g CARBOHYDRATE
37g PROTEIN	8g FAT	1.0g FIBER

Setting: HIGH

Cooking Time: 5 minutes

Utensil: 8 cups (2 L) rectangular dish

4	slices fast-fry back bacon
4	rings yellow pepper
4	thick slices tomato
4	slices Camembert or Brie cheese

Arrange bacon in rectangular dish; top each with ring of yellow pepper.

Cover loosely with plastic wrap and microwave 3 minutes.

Add tomato slices and cheese; finish microwaving 2 minutes covered.

Serve as snack or for breakfast.

Bacon Potato Treats

(serves 4)

1 SERVING	379 CALORIES	28g CARBOHYDRATE
26g PROTEIN	25g FAT	1.0g FIBER

Setting: HIGH

Cooking Time: 10 minutes

Utensil: 8 cups (2 L) rectangular dish

5	potatoes, unpeeled, sliced ½ in (1.2 cm) thick
1	onion, grated and cooked
24	stuffed green olives, chopped
½ tsp	(2 ml) chopped jalapeno
6	slices crisp bacon, chopped
1½ cups	(375 ml) grated Gruyère cheese
	salt and pepper

Arrange slices of potato in rectangular dish — this may require a couple of layers depending on the size of potatoes. Cover dish with plastic wrap and microwave 4 minutes. Rotate and microwave another 4 minutes.

When potatoes are cooked, top with grated onion. Mix olives with jalapeno and sprinkle over; add bacon and cheese.

Season very well and microwave 2 minutes uncovered. Serve as an afternoon snack or at lunchtime.

Watercress and Leek Soup

(serves 4)

1 SERVING	202 CALORIES	22g CARBOHYDRATE
8g PROTEIN	8g FAT	trace FIBER

Setting: HIGH

Cooking Time: 23 minutes

Utensil: 12 cups (2.8 L) casserole with cover

2 tbsp	(30 ml) butter
2	green onions, chopped
1	large leek, white part only, chopped
3 tbsp	(45 ml) flour
4	medium potatoes, peeled and sliced
4 cups	(1 L) hot chicken stock
¼ tsp	(1 ml) thyme
¼ tsp	(1 ml) anise
1	bunch fresh watercress, chopped
	salt and pepper

Place butter, onions and leek in casserole. Cover and microwave 4 minutes.

Mix in flour, salt and pepper. Microwave 4 minutes uncovered.

Add potatoes, chicken stock and seasonings; cover and microwave 7 minutes.

Stir well. Add watercress, season, and microwave 5 minutes covered.

Remove cover; finish microwaving 3 minutes.

1 Open leek by cutting it in 4 lengthwise. Do not, however, cut through the base. Wash well in cold water.

3 After the onions and leek have been microwaved 4 minutes, sprinkle in flour, salt and pepper. Mix well and continue microwaving 4 minutes uncovered.

2 Depending on the recipe you can use the entire leek or as in this recipe, discard the green portion and use only the white part. In either case check that sand has all been washed away.

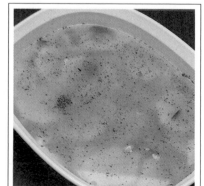

4 Add potatoes, chicken stock and seasonings; cover and microwave 7 minutes.

Green Soup

(serves 4)

1 SERVING	260 CALORIES	24g CARBOHYDRATE
12g PROTEIN	14g FAT	2.0g FIBER

Setting: HIGH

Cooking Time: 19 minutes

Utensil: 12 cups (2.8 L) casserole with cover

3 tbsp	(45 ml) butter
1	small onion, chopped
2	small stalks broccoli, pared and diced
5 tbsp	(75 ml) flour
2 cups	(500 ml) hot chicken stock
1 tsp	(5 ml) basil
2 tbsp	(30 ml) tomato paste
2 cups	(500 ml) hot milk
1	large head broccoli, in flowerets
	salt and pepper
	dash paprika

Place butter, onion and diced broccoli stalks in casserole. Cover and microwave 3 minutes.

Mix in flour and season with salt, pepper and paprika; mix very well with wooden spoon. Cover and microwave 3 minutes.

Stir in chicken stock and basil; correct seasoning. Add tomato paste and mix well. Cover and continue microwaving 4 minutes.

Pour in milk and mix well; cover and microwave another 4 minutes.

Add broccoli flowerets, cover and finish microwaving 5 minutes.

1 After 3 minutes of microwaving, add flour to vegetables. Sprinkle in paprika and season to taste.

3 Stir in chicken stock and basil; correct seasoning. Add tomato paste and mix well. Continue microwaving 4 minutes.

2 Mix well with wooden spoon. Cover and microwave 3 minutes.

4 Pour in milk. Add broccoli flowerets. Cover and finish microwaving 5 minutes.

Squash and Macaroni Soup

(serves 4)

1 SERVING	136 CALORIES	15g CARBOHYDRATE
8g PROTEIN	5g FAT	2.0g FIBER

Setting: HIGH

Cooking Time: 18 minutes

Utensil: 12 cups (2.8 L) casserole with cover

1 tbsp	(15 ml) butter
1	leek, washed and thinly sliced
½	squash, seeded and diced small
1	carrot, pared and thinly sliced
1	zucchini, peeled and sliced
5 cups	(1.2 L) hot chicken stock
1	bay leaf
¼ tsp	(1 ml) thyme
½ tsp	(2 ml) basil
½ cup	(125 ml) elbow macaroni
	salt and pepper

Place butter, leek and squash in casserole. Cover and microwave 6 minutes.

Add remaining ingredients; cover and microwave 12 minutes.

Serve hot.

Red Pepper Soup

(serves 4)

1 SERVING	141 CALORIES	16g CARBOHYDRATE
5g PROTEIN	7g FAT	1.0g FIBER

Setting: HIGH

Cooking Time: 20 minutes

Utensil: 12 cups (2.8 L) casserole with cover

2 tbsp	(30 ml) butter
1	celery stalk, diced
2	green onions, diced
4 tbsp	(60 ml) flour
2	large red peppers, seeded and sliced
2 cups	(500 ml) tomato clam juice, heated
2 cups	(500 ml) chicken stock, heated
¼ tsp	(1 ml) celery seed
1 tsp	(5 ml) sugar
	salt and pepper

Place butter, celery and onions in casserole; microwave 4 minutes covered.

Mix in flour; microwave 4 minutes covered.

Add red peppers and remaining ingredients; mix well. Cover and finish microwaving 12 minutes.

Transfer soup to food processor and purée.

Fennel Soup

(serves 4)

1 SERVING	246 CALORIES	11g CARBOHYDRATE
7g PROTEIN	20g FAT	trace FIBER

Setting: HIGH

Cooking Time: 22 minutes

Utensil: 12 cups (2.8 L) casserole with cover

4 tbsp	(60 ml) butter
1	leek, slit lengthwise in 4, washed and thinly sliced
1	medium fennel bulb, leaves and bulb thinly sliced
5 tbsp	(75 ml) flour
4 cups	(1 L) hot light chicken stock
½ cup	(125 ml) hot light cream
	pinch chervil
	salt and pepper
	lemon juice

Place butter, leek and fennel in casserole. Cover and microwave 10 minutes.

Mix well and add remaining ingredients, except cream. Continue microwaving 10 minutes covered.

Force mixture through fine sieve or food mill; stir in cream and replace in casserole. Microwave 2 minutes uncovered.

Serve hot.

Country Soup

(serves 4)

1 SERVING	289 CALORIES	11g CARBOHYDRATE
32g PROTEIN	12g FAT	1.0g FIBER

Setting: HIGH

Cooking Time: 48 minutes

Utensil: 12 cups (2.8 L) casserole with cover

2 tbsp	(30 ml) butter
1	celery stalk, diced
1	carrot, pared and diced
1	medium onion, diced
1	garlic clove, smashed and chopped
½ tsp	(2 ml) chervil
1	bay leaf
½ cup	(125 ml) yellow split peas
½ lb	(250 g) flank steak, thinly sliced and seared in oil
5 cups	(1.2 L) light beef stock, heated
6	large mushrooms, diced
	salt and pepper

Place butter, celery, carrot, onion, garlic, seasonings and bay leaf in casserole; cover and microwave 5 minutes.

Mix in peas, meat and beef stock; correct seasoning. Cover and continue microwaving 40 minutes.

Stir in mushrooms and finish microwaving 3 minutes uncovered.

Potato Onion Cream

(serves 4)

1 SERVING	313 CALORIES	42g CARBOHYDRATE
15g PROTEIN	11g FAT	1.0g FIBER

Setting: MEDIUM-HIGH and MEDIUM

Cooking Time: 31 minutes

Utensil: 12 cups (2.8 L) casserole with cover

2	slices bacon, diced
3	medium onions, diced
4 tbsp	(60 ml) flour
4 cups	(1 L) hot milk
3	large potatoes, peeled and thinly sliced
1 tsp	(5 ml) tarragon
	salt and white pepper
	dash paprika

Place bacon and onions in casserole; cover and microwave 6 minutes at MEDIUM-HIGH.

Mix in flour. Pour in milk, stir, and add tarragon, salt, pepper and paprika.

Add potatoes and cover. Microwave 14 minutes at MEDIUM-HIGH.

Stir mixture well and microwave 11 minutes at MEDIUM, covered.

Serve hot.

Thick Leftover Vegetable Soup

(serves 4)

1 SERVING	289 CALORIES	27g CARBOHYDRATE
20g PROTEIN	11g FAT	1.0g FIBER

Setting: HIGH

Cooking Time: 23 minutes

Utensil: 12 cups (2.8 L) casserole with cover

2 tbsp	(30 ml) butter
2	leeks, white part only, thinly sliced
1	garlic clove, smashed and chopped
1	green pepper, diced
2	potatoes, peeled, quartered and thinly sliced
1	large sweet potato, peeled, quartered and thinly sliced
½ tsp	(2 ml) basil
¼ tsp	(1 ml) celery seed
¼ tsp	(1 ml) anise
5 cups	(1.2 L) hot chicken stock
1 cup	(250 ml) diced cooked chicken
	salt and pepper

Place butter in casserole; cover and microwave 1 minute. Add leeks and continue microwaving 5 minutes covered.

Stir in garlic and green pepper; season well. Cover and microwave 3 minutes.

Stir and add potatoes, sweet potato and seasonings; cover and microwave 3 minutes.

Pour in chicken stock; mix well and microwave 10 minutes uncovered.

Add diced chicken and correct seasoning. Finish microwaving 1 minute with cover.

Perch Soup

(serves 4)

1 SERVING	209 CALORIES	23g CARBOHYDRATE
21g PROTEIN	4g FAT	2.0g FIBER

Setting: MEDIUM-HIGH and MEDIUM

Cooking Time: 31 minutes

Utensil: 12 cups (2.8 L) casserole with cover

2	slices bacon, diced
1	celery stalk, diced
1	garlic clove, smashed and chopped
4 tbsp	(60 ml) flour
4 cups	(1 L) light chicken stock, heated
2	large potatoes, peeled and diced
¼ tsp	(1 ml) fennel
1 tsp	(5 ml) chopped parsley
1	bay leaf
½ tsp	(2 ml) thyme
2	perch filets, cubed
1	red pepper, diced
	salt and pepper

Place bacon, celery and garlic in casserole. Cover and microwave 5 minutes at MEDIUM-HIGH.

Mix in flour, pour in chicken stock and mix again. Add potatoes, fennel, parsley, bay leaf and thyme. Cover and microwave 20 minutes at MEDIUM-HIGH; stir once during this time.

Mix in fish and red pepper; correct seasoning. Microwave 6 minutes at MEDIUM uncovered.

Serve hot.

Chicken Casserole

(serves 4)

1 SERVING	361 CALORIES	22g CARBOHYDRATE
31g PROTEIN	16g FAT	1.0g FIBER

Setting: HIGH

Cooking Time: 16 minutes

Utensil: 12 cups (2.8 L) casserole with cover

4 tbsp	(60 ml) butter
2	potatoes, peeled and cubed
2	carrots, pared and cubed
2	celery stalks, pared and cubed
1 tbsp	(15 ml) chopped fresh parsley
2	chicken breasts, skinned, halved and boned
¼ tsp	(1 ml) anise
3 tbsp	(45 ml) flour
1½ cups	(375 ml) hot chicken stock
1 cup	(250 ml) cooked pearl onions
	salt and pepper

Place butter, potatoes, carrots, celery and parsley in casserole. Cover and microwave 8 minutes.

Add chicken breasts and anise; season generously.

Mix in flour until well incorporated. Pour in chicken stock, cover and microwave 6 minutes.

Stir in onions and microwave 2 minutes uncovered.

Place butter, potatoes, carrots, celery and parsley in casserole. Cover and microwave 8 minutes.

Add chicken breasts and anise; season generously.

Check if vegetables are cooked by piercing with knife.

Mix in flour until well incorporated.

Chicken and Shrimp Casserole

(serves 4)

1 SERVING	644 CALORIES	35g CARBOHYDRATE
84g PROTEIN	13g FAT	1.0g FIBER

Setting: MEDIUM-HIGH

Cooking Time: 10 minutes

Utensil: 12 cups (2.8 L) casserole with cover

2 tbsp	(30 ml) butter
1 tbsp	(15 ml) chopped shallot
1 lb	(500 g) mushrooms, diced
24	large shrimp, shelled and deveined
2	chicken breasts, skinned, halved, boned, meat cut in 1 in (2.5 cm) chunks
2 cups	(500 ml) cooked elbow macaroni
1 cup	(250 ml) grated mozzarella cheese
½ cup	(125 ml) tomato sauce, heated
1 cup	(250 ml) brown sauce, heated
	salt and pepper

Place butter, shallot, mushrooms, shrimp and chicken in casserole. Cover and microwave 5 minutes.

Season well and mix. Add remaining ingredients and finish microwaving 5 minutes covered.

Serve with green salad.

Chicken and Melon Casserole

(serves 4)

1 SERVING	334 CALORIES	14g CARBOHYDRATE
30g PROTEIN	13g FAT	1.0g FIBER

Setting: HIGH

Cooking Time: 13 minutes

Utensil: 12 cups (2.8 L) casserole with cover

3 tbsp	(45 ml) butter
2	chicken breasts, skinned, halved, boned, and cut in large pieces
1 tbsp	(15 ml) chopped parsley
1 tsp	(5 ml) tarragon
1	celery stalk, sliced
20	mushrooms, halved
3 tbsp	(45 ml) flour
1¼ cups	(300 ml) beer
1	cantaloupe melon, cut in half
	salt and pepper

Place butter and chicken in casserole. Add parsley, tarragon, celery, salt and pepper. Cover and microwave 6 minutes.

Add mushrooms and mix in flour; pour in beer. Microwave 6 minutes uncovered.

Using melon-ball cutter, scoop out melon flesh and add to casserole. Mix very well and finish microwaving 1 minute uncovered.

Chicken Chili

(serves 4)

1 SERVING	387 CALORIES	37g CARBOHYDRATE
31g PROTEIN	13g FAT	2.0g FIBER

Setting: HIGH

Cooking Time: 95 minutes

Utensil: 12 cups (2.8 L) casserole with cover

1 tbsp	(15 ml) butter
1	onion, chopped
2	celery stalks, chopped
1	small leek, washed and chopped
1½ cups	(375 ml) diced raw chicken, dark meat preferably
3 cups	(750 ml) white beans, soaked in water overnight
¼ tsp	(1 ml) crushed chillies
½ tsp	(2 ml) oregano
½ tsp	(2 ml) cumin
½ tsp	(2 ml) allspice
2	hot banana peppers
	hot chicken stock
	salt and pepper
	grated mozzarella cheese

Place butter, onion, celery, leek, salt and pepper in casserole. Cover and microwave 5 minutes.

Mix well and add raw chicken, beans (with liquid), seasonings and banana peppers. Pour in enough hot chicken stock to cover by 2 in (5 cm). Cover casserole and microwave 75 minutes. Stir at least 2 or 3 times.

Note: At some point during this cooking time the banana peppers must be removed. The exact time will depend on how spicy you desire the chili — leaving them in 15 minutes will produce a medium-hot flavor.

Also, if at any time the chicken stock reduces considerably, add more.

Stir in mozzarella cheese to taste and correct seasoning. Cover and finish microwaving beans 15 minutes.

Meat and Potato Casserole

(serves 4)

1 SERVING	473 CALORIES	33g CARBOHYDRATE
61g PROTEIN	11g FAT	2.0g FIBER

Setting: HIGH
Cooking Time: 25 minutes
Utensil: 12 cups (2.8 L) casserole with cover

1 tbsp	(15 ml) butter
½	red onion, finely chopped
1½ lb	(750 g) lean ground beef
¼ tsp	(1 ml) chili powder
¼ tsp	(1 ml) allspice
½ tsp	(2 ml) thyme
3	potatoes, peeled and thinly sliced
¼ tsp	(1 ml) paprika
28 oz	(796 ml) can tomatoes, drained and chopped
1 cup	(250 ml) tomato sauce, heated
	salt and pepper
	chopped parsley to taste

Place butter, onion and meat in casserole. Season well with chili powder, allspice and thyme. Cover and microwave 6 minutes.

Mix well and cover with ½ of sliced potatoes; sprinkle with paprika.

Add tomatoes, tomato sauce and chopped parsley. Cover with remaining potatoes and season well.

Cover and microwave 12 minutes

Mix well and continue microwaving 7 minutes covered.

Place butter, onion and meat in casserole. Season well with chili powder, allspice and thyme. Cover and microwave 6 minutes.

Mix well and cover with ½ of sliced potatoes; sprinkle with paprika.

Add tomatoes, tomato sauce and parsley.

Cover with remaining potatoes and season well. Cover and microwave 12 minutes. Stir and finish microwaving 7 minutes.

Ground Veal Casserole

(serves 4)

1 SERVING	498 CALORIES	15g CARBOHYDRATE
55g PROTEIN	24g FAT	2.0g FIBER

Setting: HIGH

Cooking Time: 10 minutes

Utensil: 12 cups (2.8 L) casserole with cover

2 tbsp	(30 ml) butter
1	medium onion, chopped
1	green pepper, diced
1	yellow pepper, diced
1 tsp	(5 ml) oregano
1½ lb	(750 g) lean ground veal
28 oz	(796 ml) can tomatoes, chopped with juice
2 tbsp	(30 ml) tomato paste
1 cup	(250 ml) diced cheddar cheese
	salt and pepper

Place butter, onion, peppers and oregano in casserole. Cover and microwave 3 minutes.

Add veal, mix and season. Continue microwaving 3 minutes covered.

Add remaining ingredients and mix well. Correct seasoning and microwave 4 minutes covered.

Serve with fresh bread.

Meaty Tomato Casserole

(serves 4)

1 SERVING	446 CALORIES	13g CARBOHYDRATE
60g PROTEIN	17g FAT	1.0g FIBER

Setting: HIGH

Cooking Time: 10 minutes

Utensil: 12 cups (2.8 L) casserole with cover

2 tbsp	(30 ml) butter
1	small onion, finely chopped
2	garlic cloves, smashed and chopped
½ lb	(250 g) mushrooms, diced
1 tbsp	(15 ml) chopped chives
½ tsp	(2 ml) chili powder
1½ lb	(750 g) lean ground beef
1½ cups	(375 ml) tomato sauce, heated
¼ cup	(50 ml) sour cream
	salt and pepper

Place butter, onion, garlic, mushrooms, chives and chili powder in casserole. Cover and microwave 4 minutes.

Season well and mix in ground beef; cover and continue microwaving 3 minutes.

Stir and pour in tomato sauce; microwave 3 minutes covered.

Remove from microwave, mix in sour cream and serve over noodles.

Leftover Casserole

(serves 4)

1 SERVING	681 CALORIES	50g CARBOHYDRATE
63g PROTEIN	24g FAT	1.0g FIBER

Setting: HIGH

Cooking Time: 7 minutes

Utensil: 12 cups (2.8 L) casserole with cover

1 lb	(500 g) leftover cooked ham, in strips
½	onion, thinly sliced
2 tbsp	(30 ml) garlic butter
2	garlic cloves, smashed and chopped
1 tbsp	(15 ml) chopped parsley
28 oz	(796 ml) can tomatoes, chopped, with ½ of juice
3 cups	(750 ml) leftover cooked macaroni
½	green pepper, thinly sliced
1 tbsp	(15 ml) tomato paste
1 cup	(250 ml) grated cheddar or other leftover cheese
	salt and pepper

Place ham, onion, garlic butter, garlic, parsley, salt and pepper in casserole. Cover and microwave 3 minutes.

Mix in tomatoes, macaroni and green pepper; season generously.

Add tomato paste and cheese; stir well. Cover and microwave 4 minutes.

Lima Bean Dinner

(serves 4)

1 SERVING	261 CALORIES	42g CARBOHYDRATE
15g PROTEIN	8g FAT	2.0g FIBER

Setting: HIGH

Cooking Time: 56½ minutes

Utensil: 12 cups (2.8 L) casserole with cover

1 tbsp	(15 ml) butter
1	medium onion, chopped
½ tsp	(2 ml) marjoram
½ tsp	(2 ml) chervil
4	slices bacon, diced
3	celery stalks, diced
14 oz	(400 g) dried lima beans, soaked in water overnight
2 tbsp	(30 ml) brown sugar
2 tbsp	(30 ml) molasses
1 tsp	(5 ml) dry mustard
1 tbsp	(15 ml) cornstarch
2 tbsp	(30 ml) cold water
	salt and pepper
	dash paprika
	hot chicken stock

Microwave butter ½ minute in casserole uncovered.

Add onion, marjoram and chervil. Cover and microwave 2 minutes.

Stir in bacon and microwave 4 minutes uncovered. Mix well; microwave another 3 minutes.

Spread celery over bacon. Cover with beans (including liquid). Sprinkle in brown sugar and molasses.

Mix in mustard and season with salt, pepper and paprika; mix again.

Pour in enough hot chicken stock to cover. Cover casserole and microwave 30 minutes.

Mix well; continue microwaving 17 minutes covered.

Mix cornstarch with water; stir into bean mixture, let stand ½ minute and serve.

Microwave onion, marjoram and chervil for 2 minutes covered.

Add celery, beans, brown sugar and molasses.

Microwave bacon a total of 7 minutes but be sure to stir about halfway through.

Mix in mustard, salt, pepper and paprika. Pour in enough chicken stock to cover. Microwave a total of 47 minutes covered, stirring once.

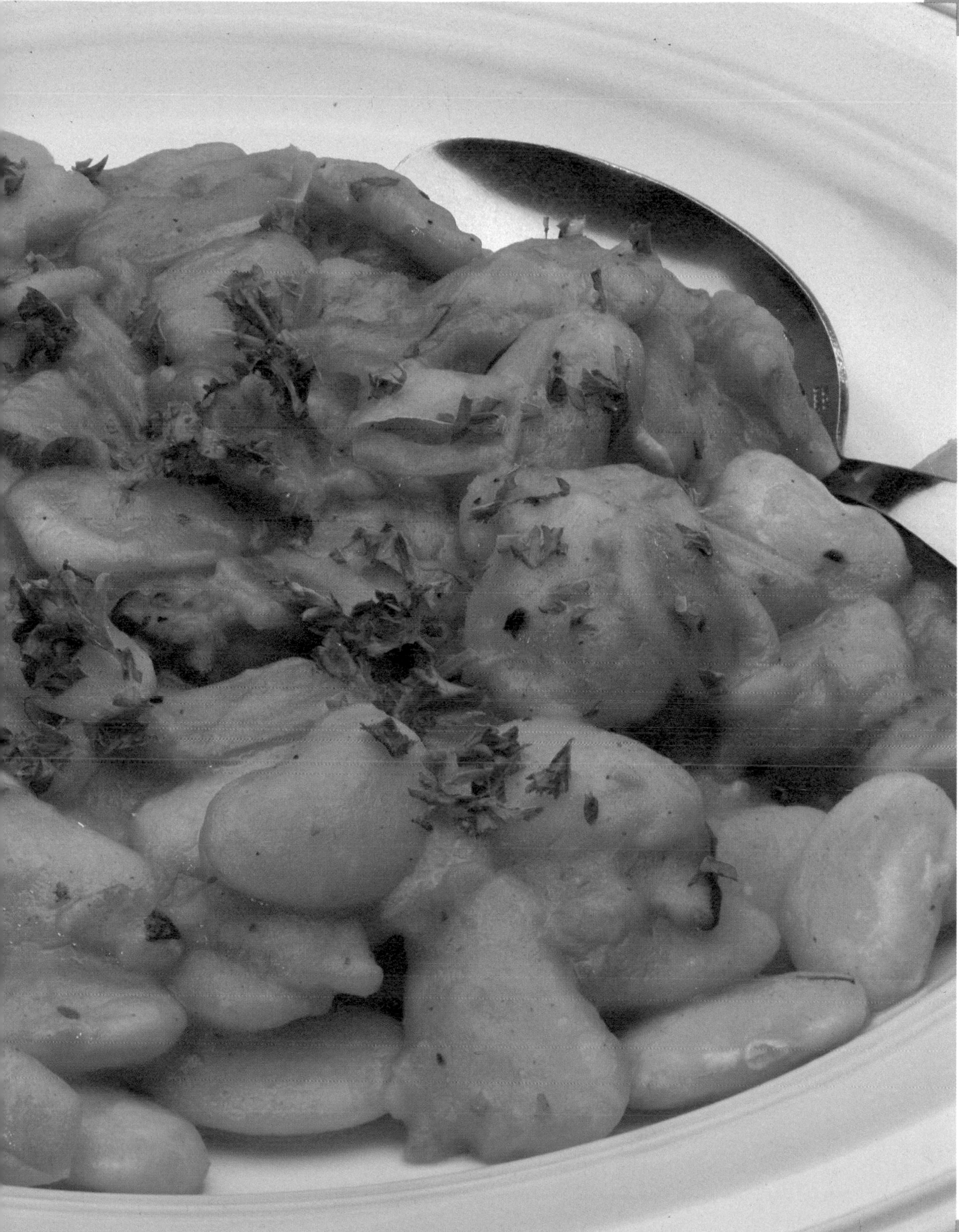

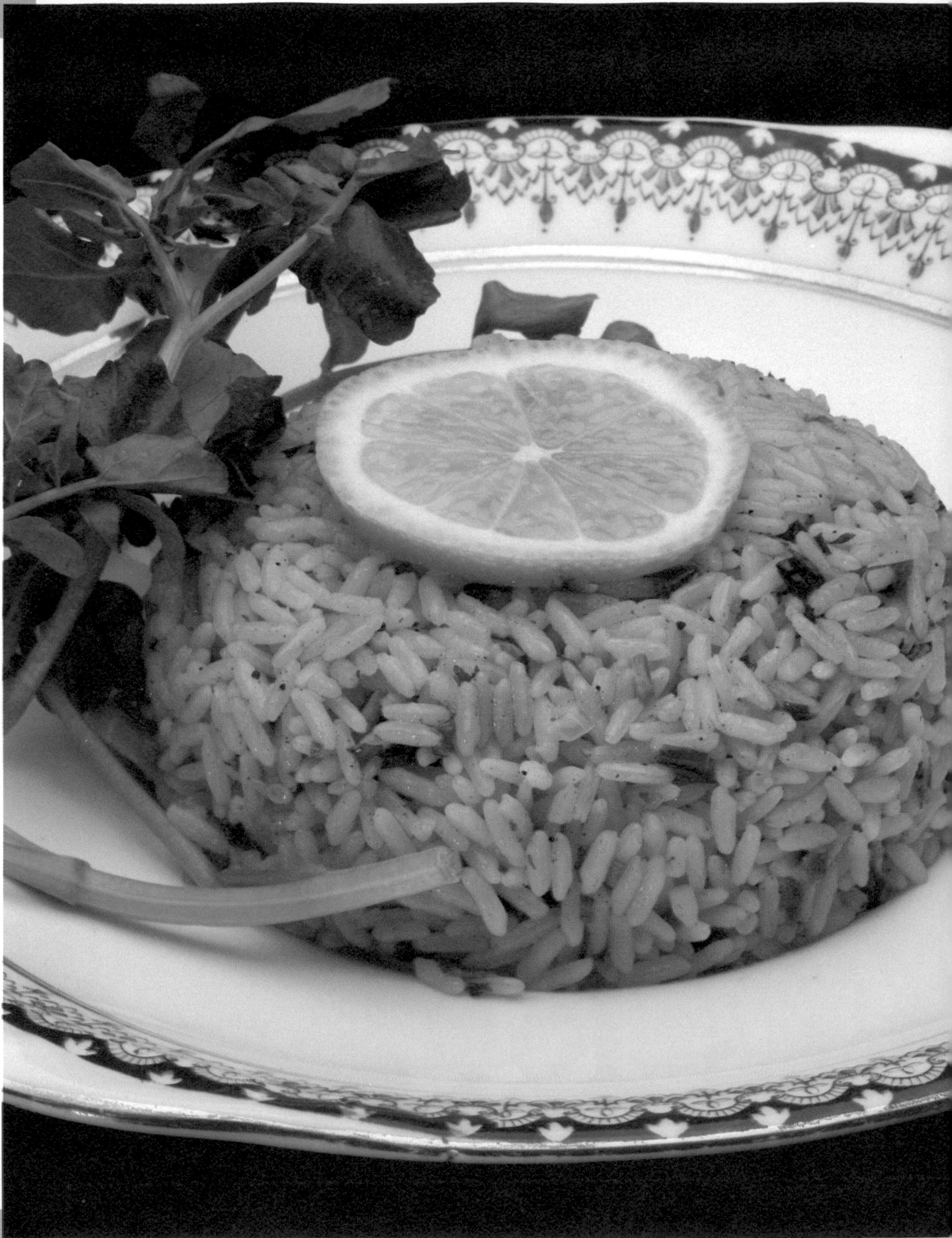

Watercress Rice

(serves 4)

1 SERVING	124 CALORIES	18g CARBOHYDRATE
4g PROTEIN	5g FAT	trace FIBER

Setting: HIGH

Cooking Time: 20½ minutes

Utensil: 12 cups (2.8 L) casserole with cover

1 tbsp	(15 ml) butter
2	green onions, chopped
½	medium white onion, chopped
1 cup	(250 ml) long grain rice, rinsed
2 cups	(500 ml) hot chicken stock
3 tbsp	(45 ml) finely chopped watercress
1 tbsp	(15 ml) chopped parsley
1 tbsp	(15 ml) chopped chives
	salt, pepper, paprika
	pinch tarragon
	butter to taste

Microwave butter ½ minute in casserole uncovered.

Add both onions; cover and microwave 2 minutes.

Stir in rice, salt, pepper and paprika. Pour in chicken stock and mix again. Cover and microwave 18 minutes, mixing halfway through.

Stir in remaining ingredients and serve.

After onions have microwaved 2 minutes, stir in rice, salt, pepper and paprika.

Pour in chicken stock and mix again. Cover and microwave 18 minutes.

Cooked rice should be moist and fluffy.

Stir in remaining ingredients and serve.

Vegetable Pasta Casserole

(serves 4)

1 SERVING	407 CALORIES	56g CARBOHYDRATE
17g PROTEIN	14g FAT	2.0g FIBER

Setting: HIGH

Cooking Time: 14 minutes

Utensil: 12 cups (2.8 L) casserole with cover

1 tbsp	(15 ml) butter
½	yellow pepper, diced large
½	red pepper, diced large
½	green pepper, diced large
1	very small eggplant, diced
3 tbsp	(45 ml) flour
1½ cups	(375 ml) hot milk
2	celery stalks, sliced
½	cucumber, peeled, seeded and sliced
8	lichees
3 cups	(750 ml) cooked medium conch shells
1 cup	(250 ml) grated mozzarella cheese
¼ tsp	(1 ml) nutmeg
¼ tsp	(1 ml) celery salt
1 cup	(250 ml) tomato sauce, heated
	salt and pepper

Place butter, peppers, eggplant, salt and pepper in casserole. Cover and microwave 4 minutes.

Mix in flour, pour in hot milk and stir well.

Mix in remaining ingredients and correct seasoning. Cover and microwave 10 minutes.

If desired decorate servings with sliced tomatoes.

Macaroni and Eggs

(serves 4)

1 SERVING	818 CALORIES	59g CARBOHYDRATE
54g PROTEIN	41g FAT	1.0g FIBER

Setting: HIGH and MEDIUM-HIGH

Cooking Time: 10 minutes

Utensil: 12 cups (2.8 L) casserole with cover

2 tbsp	(30 ml) butter
⅓ lb	(150 g) mushrooms, diced
1 tsp	(5 ml) chopped parsley
1	shallot, chopped
4 cups	(1 L) leftover cooked macaroni
5	hard-boiled eggs, sliced
1½ cups	(375 ml) diced cooked ham
1 cup	(250 ml) grated Gruyère cheese
2½ cups	(625 ml) hot light white sauce
	salt and pepper
	few drops lemon juice

Place butter, mushrooms, parsley, shallot, salt, pepper and lemon juice in casserole. Cover and microwave 4 minutes at HIGH.

Drain mushrooms, reserving liquid, and set aside.

Spread ½ of macaroni in bottom of casserole. Top with all sliced eggs.

Cover with ham and drained mushrooms; top with ½ of cheese. Add remaining macaroni.

Mix reserved cooking liquid from mushrooms with white sauce. Pour this over macaroni and finish with grated cheese.

Cover casserole and microwave 6 minutes at MEDIUM-HIGH.

Scallop Salad

(serves 4)

SERVING	395 CALORIES	8g CARBOHYDRATE
0g PROTEIN	31g FAT	1.0g FIBER

Setting: MEDIUM-HIGH
Cooking Time: 3 minutes
Utensil: 12 cups (2.8 L)
casserole with cover

1 lb	(500 g) sea scallops
2 tbsp	(30 ml) lime juice
1 tbsp	(15 ml) butter
¼ tsp	(1 ml) anise seed
¼ cup	(50 ml) dry white wine
1	celery stalk, sliced
½ cup	(125 ml) radishes, thinly sliced
2	green onions, chopped
1 tbsp	(15 ml) Dijon mustard
3 tbsp	(45 ml) raspberry wine vinegar
½ cup	(125 ml) olive oil
	salt and fresh ground pepper
	lemon juice
	few drops Tabasco sauce

Place scallops, lime juice, butter, anise seed, wine and pepper in casserole. Cover and microwave 3 minutes.

Drain scallops and transfer to bowl. Mix in celery, radishes and onions; set aside.

In second bowl, whisk mustard, vinegar, salt and pepper together.

Incorporate oil in thin stream while whisking constantly. Correct seasoning, add lemon juice and Tabasco sauce and pour vinaigrette over salad to taste.

Toss and serve.

Haddock Casserole

(serves 4)

1 SERVING	414 CALORIES	45g CARBOHYDRATE
25g PROTEIN	15g FAT	2.0g FIBER

Setting: HIGH

Cooking Time: 21 minutes

Utensil: 12 cups (2.8 L) casserole with cover

4 tbsp	(60 ml) butter
2	celery stalks, sliced thick
1	onion, in chunks
1	fennel bulb, cut in ½ and cubed
5 tbsp	(75 ml) flour
3 cups	(750 ml) hot chicken stock
10 oz	(300 g) haddock filets, cut in 1 in (1.5 cm) wide strips
8	small round potatoes, peeled and cooked*
1	sweet potato, peeled, cooked and cubed*
	salt and pepper

Place butter, celery, onion and fennel in casserole; season well. Cover and microwave 5 minutes.

Mix in flour. Cover and microwave 2 minutes.

Pour in chicken stock, mix and microwave 5 minutes uncovered. Stir well; continue microwaving 5 minutes uncovered.

Correct seasoning and add fish, potatoes and sweet potato. Microwave 4 minutes uncovered.

* The canned variety serves as an excellent substitute for fresh produce.

Place butter, celery, onion and fennel in casserole; season well. Cover and microwave 5 minutes.

Mix in flour. Cover and microwave 2 minutes.

Pour in chicken stock, mix and microwave 5 minute uncovered. Stir well; continue microwaving 5 minutes uncovered

Correct seasoning and add fish, potatoes and sweet potatocs. Microwave 4 minute uncovered.

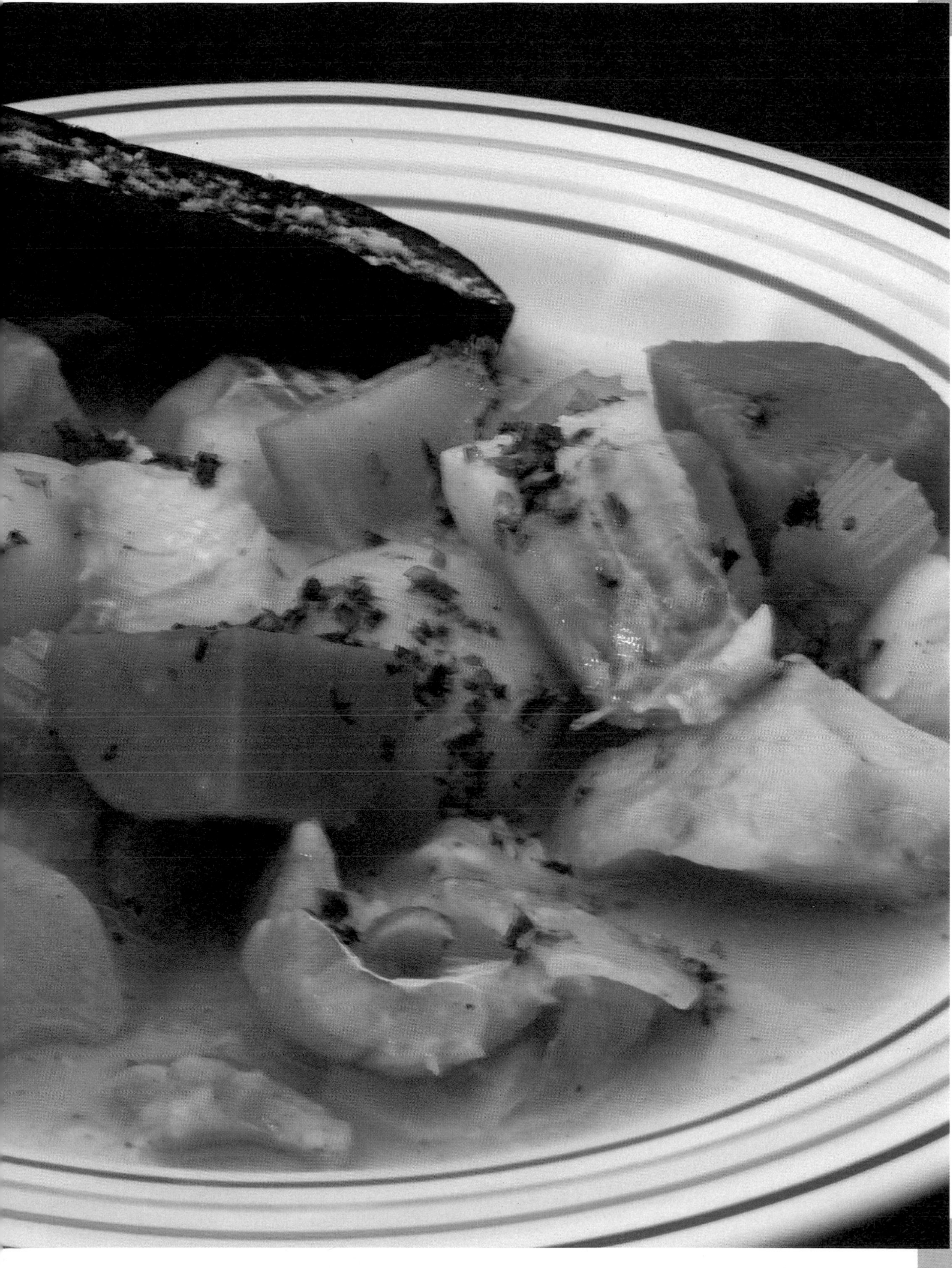

Shrimp Bisque

(serves 4)

1 SERVING	315 CALORIES	13g CARBOHYDRATE
24g PROTEIN	20g FAT	trace FIBER

Setting: HIGH

Cooking Time: 25 minutes

Utensil: 12 cups (2.8 L) casserole with cover

4 tbsp	(60 ml) butter
1	carrot, pared and diced small
1	celery stalk, diced small
1	shallot, chopped
12	large shrimp, unpeeled
¼ tsp	(1 ml) fennel
1 tsp	(5 ml) chopped chives
5 tbsp	(75 ml) flour
4 cups	(1 L) hot fish stock
½ cup	(125 ml) hot light cream
	salt and pepper

Place butter, vegetables, shallot, shrimp, salt and pepper in casserole. Cover and microwave 8 minutes.

Remove shrimp from casserole and shell. Set shrimp and shells aside.

Add seasonings and flour to vegetables in casserole; mix well. Place shrimp shells and fish stock in casserole. Cover and microwave 15 minutes.

Pass mixture through sieve using pestle and pour back into casserole.

Chop shrimp and stir into soup. Add cream and season to taste. Microwave 2 minutes uncovered.

Boston Bluefish with Vegetables

(serves 4)

1 SERVING	169 CALORIES	8g CARBOHYDRATE
19g PROTEIN	6g FAT	1.0g FIBER

Setting: HIGH and MEDIUM-HIGH

Cooking Time: 12 minutes

Utensil: 12 cups (2.8 L) casserole with cover

1	leek, cut in 4 lengthwise, washed and chopped
1 tbsp	(15 ml) chopped parsley
1 tbsp	(15 ml) butter
¼ tsp	(1 ml) fennel
12 oz	(350 g) Boston Bluefish filets
8	lichees nuts
2	tomatoes, sliced
	salt and pepper

Place leek, parsley, butter and fennel in casserole. Cover and microwave 4 minutes at HIGH.

Lay filets in casserole; add lichees and tomato slices. Cover and microwave 5 minutes at MEDIUM-HIGH.

Turn filets over and correct seasoning. Cover and microwave 3 minutes at MEDIUM-HIGH.

Grilled Rainbow Trout

(serves 2)

1 SERVING	370 CALORIES	1g CARBOHYDRATE
28g PROTEIN	27g FAT	--g FIBER

Setting: HIGH

Cooking Time: 5½ minutes

Utensil: 12 cups (2.8 L) casserole with cover

1 tbsp	(15 ml) butter
2	rainbow trout, gutted and cleaned
	lime juice
	salt and pepper
	melted butter
	toasted slivered almonds

Place butter in casserole and microwave ½ minute uncovered.

Season insides of trout with lime juice, salt and pepper. Place in casserole, cover and microwave 3 minutes.

Turn trout over; continue microwaving 2 minutes covered.

Serve with melted butter and garnish with slivered almonds.

Vermouth Scallops

(serves 4)

1 SERVING	336 CALORIES	14g CARBOHYDRATE
28g PROTEIN	17g FAT	1.0g FIBER

Setting: MEDIUM-HIGH and HIGH

Cooking Time: 11 minutes

Utensil: 12 cups (2.8 L) casserole with cover
4 individual microwave coquille dishes

1 lb	(500 g) fresh scallops
3 tbsp	(45 ml) butter
1 tbsp	(15 ml) chopped parsley
½ lb	(250 g) mushrooms, quartered
1 tbsp	(15 ml) lime juice

3 tbsp	(45 ml) dry vermouth
3 tbsp	(45 ml) flour
½ cup	(125 ml) hot milk
¼ tsp	(1 ml) fennel seed
1 cup	(250 ml) grated mozzarella cheese
	salt and pepper
	dash paprika
	few drops lemon juice

Place scallops, butter, parsley, mushrooms and lime juice in casserole.

Pour in vermouth, cover and microwave 3 minutes at MEDIUM-HIGH.

Mix in flour. Continue microwaving 3 minutes, covered, at MEDIUM-HIGH.

Remove scallops and set aside.

Add hot milk, fennel, salt, pepper and paprika to casserole; mix well and sprinkle in lemon juice to taste. Microwave 4 minutes at HIGH uncovered.

Replace scallops in casserole and mix well. Spoon mixture into coquille dishes and top with cheese; microwave 1 minute at HIGH uncovered.

Place scallops, butter, parsley, mushrooms and lime juice in casserole.

Mix in flour. Continue microwaving 3 minutes covered at MEDIUM-HIGH.

Pour in vermouth, cover and microwave 3 minutes at MEDIUM-HIGH.

Remove scallops and set aside.

Haddock Topped with Cheese

(serves 4)

1 SERVING	166 CALORIES	2g CARBOHYDRATE
21g PROTEIN	7g FAT	trace FIBER

Setting: MEDIUM-HIGH

Cooking Time: 8 minutes

Utensil: 12 cups (2.8 L) casserole with cover Microwave serving platter

12.3 oz	(350 g) package frozen haddock filets
1 tbsp	(15 ml) lime or lemon juice
3	green onions, chopped
1 tbsp	(15 ml) butter
¼ tsp	(1 ml) fennel seed
¼ tsp	(1 ml) tarragon
½ cup	(125 ml) grated mozzarella cheese
	salt and pepper
	paprika to taste

Grease casserole and add frozen fish, lime juice and onions.

Sprinkle in butter, fennel seed and tarragon; season well. Cover and microwave 5 minutes.

Turn filets over; cover and continue microwaving 2 minutes.

Transfer fish to serving platter, season with paprika and top with cheese. Finish microwaving 1 minute uncovered.

Serve with small salad and vegetables.

Use fish straight from the freezer.

Place frozen fish, lime juice and onions in greased casserole. Add butter, fennel seed and tarragon; season well. Cover and microwave 5 minutes.

Turn filets over; cover and continue microwaving 2 minutes.

Transfer fish to serving platter, season with paprika and top with cheese. Finish microwaving 1 minute uncovered.

Oyster Bake

(serves 4)

1 SERVING	390 CALORIES	10g CARBOHYDRATE
48g PROTEIN	16g FAT	trace FIBER

Setting: HIGH
Cooking Time: 13 minutes
Utensil: 8 cups (2 L) rectangular dish

2 tbsp	(30 ml) butter
4	large sole filets
1 tbsp	(15 ml) chopped shallot
1 tbsp	(15 ml) chopped parsley
24	shrimp, shelled and deveined
1 cup	(250 ml) halved mushrooms
1 cup	(250 ml) shucked oysters
½ cup	(125 ml) dry white wine
½ cup	(125 ml) hot light cream
	pinch fennel
	salt and pepper
	lemon juice

Place half of butter and all filets in rectangular dish. Season well and cover with pierced plastic wrap; microwave 3 minutes.

Turn filets over and continue microwaving 4 minutes covered.

Remove fish and transfer to serving platter; set aside.

Add remaining butter, shallot, parsley, shrimp and mushrooms to rectangular dish; cover with plastic wrap and microwave 4 minutes.

Season well with fennel, salt, pepper and lemon juice. Add oysters and wine; mix well. Cover and continue microwaving 2 minutes.

Stir in cream and correct seasoning.

Pour over fish and serve.

Scampi Parisienne

(serves 4)

1 SERVING	494 CALORIES	23g CARBOHYDRATE
66g PROTEIN	15g FAT	1.0g FIBER

Setting: HIGH
Cooking Time: 5½ minutes
Utensil: 12 cups (2.8 L) casserole with cover

4 tbsp	(60 ml) butter
32	scampi, shelled
2	garlic cloves, smashed and chopped
1 cup	(250 ml) water chestnuts
1 cup	(250 ml) cooked Parisienne potatoes
2	tomatoes, peeled and diced
1 tbsp	(15 ml) chopped parsley or chives
1 tsp	(5 ml) soya sauce
1 tsp	(5 ml) chopped pickled banana pepper
	salt and pepper

Place butter in casserole and microwave ½ minute uncovered.

Add scampi and garlic; season well. Cover and microwave 2 minutes.

Mix in remaining ingredients and correct seasoning. Finish microwaving 3 minutes covered.

Ocean Perch and Cabbage

(serves 4)

1 SERVING	228 CALORIES	11g CARBOHYDRATE
31g PROTEIN	6g FAT	1.0g FIBER

Setting: MEDIUM-HIGH

Cooking Time: 12 minutes

Utensil: 12 cups (2.8 L) casserole with cover

½	cabbage, thinly sliced, cooked
4 tbsp	(60 ml) grated Parmesan cheese
4	ocean perch filets
2 tsp	(10 ml) butter
½ tsp	(2 ml) fennel seeds
¼ tsp	(1 ml) anise
¼ tsp	(1 ml) paprika
14 oz	(398 ml) tomato sauce, heated
	salt and pepper

Lightly grease casserole. Add half of cabbage and top with half of cheese.

Add filets flat and dot with butter. Sprinkle in seasonings followed by remaining cheese and cabbage.

Season again with salt and pepper and pour in tomato sauce. Cover and microwave 12 minutes.

Serve with spaghetti squash.

Baked Apples

(serves 4)

1 SERVING	87 CALORIES	11g CARBOHYDRATE
trace PROTEIN	2g FAT	1.0g FIBER

Setting: HIGH

Cooking Time: 9 minutes

Utensil: 8 cups (2 L) casserole with cover

2	apples, hollowed
2 tsp	(10 ml) butter
½ tsp	(2 ml) cinnamon
	lemon juice

Using small knife score apples around middle to prevent skin from splitting during cooking.

Place apples in casserole and sprinkle remaining ingredients over. Cover and microwave 9 minutes.

When apples are cooked, cut each into half and serve as garnish with flounder filets.

Pineapple Flounder Filets

(serves 4)

1 SERVING	163 CALORIES	8g CARBOHYDRATE
15g PROTEIN	4g FAT	1.0g FIBER

Setting: HIGH and MEDIUM-HIGH

Cooking Time: 6 minutes

Utensil: 8 cups (2 L) rectangular dish

1 tbsp	(15 ml) butter
4	flounder filets
1 tbsp	(15 ml) chopped parsley
1	yellow pepper, thinly sliced
4	fresh pineapple rings
	salt and pepper
	dash paprika
	lemon juice

Arrange all ingredients in rectangular dish and cover with pierced plastic wrap; microwave 4 minutes at HIGH.

Turn filets over and continue microwaving 2 minutes at MEDIUM-HIGH, covered with plastic wrap.

Serve with baked apples.

Sweet, Sweet Potatoes

(serves 4)

1 SERVING	173 CALORIES	41g CARBOHYDRATE
2g PROTEIN	trace FAT	1.0g FIBER

Setting: HIGH

Cooking Time: 23 minutes

Utensil: Stoneware serving platter

2	large sweet potatoes
1 tbsp	(15 ml) brown sugar
1 tsp	(5 ml) cinnamon
¼ cup	(50 ml) orange juice
2 tbsp	(30 ml) molasses

Wrap each potato in plastic wrap, prick several times and place in microwave. Microwave 20 minutes depending on size, turning 3 to 4 times.

Remove and slice with skin about ½ in (1.2 cm) thick. Arrange pieces on stoneware plate and top with remaining ingredients. Microwave 1½ minutes uncovered.

Turn pieces over; continue microwaving another 1½ minutes uncovered.

Garlicky Sweet Potatoes

(serves 4)

1 SERVING	349 CALORIES	62g CARBOHYDRATE
12g PROTEIN	6g FAT	2.0g FIBER

Setting: HIGH
Cooking Time: 23 minutes
Utensil: None

4	large sweet potatoes
3	slices crisp bacon, chopped
2	garlic cloves, smashed and chopped
1 tbsp	(15 ml) chopped parsley
½ cup	(125 ml) cooked shrimp, chopped
4 tbsp	(60 ml) sour cream
	salt and pepper

Wrap each potato in plastic wrap; prick each several times with knife. Place in microwave for 8 minutes.

Turn potatoes over; continue microwaving 15 minutes. Remove and unwrap.

Mix remaining ingredients together; season to taste.

Slit potatoes open and top with mixture. Serve.

Endive Ham Bake

(serves 4)

1 SERVING	350 CALORIES	11g CARBOHYDRATE
26g PROTEIN	11g FAT	1.0g FIBER

Setting: HIGH
Cooking Time: 23 minutes
Utensil: 12 cups (2.8 L) casserole with cover

4	endives
2 tbsp	(30 ml) butter
1 tbsp	(15 ml) lemon juice
1 tbsp	(15 ml) chopped parsley
½ tsp	(2 ml) tarragon
½ cup	(125 ml) light chicken stock
4	large slices Black Forest ham, fat removed
1½ cups	(375 ml) light white sauce, heated
1 cup	(250 ml) grated mozzarella cheese
	salt and pepper

Slit endives in four lengthwise without cutting through the base. Wash well in cold water and shake off excess.

Place endives, butter, lemon juice, parsley, tarragon and chicken stock in casserole; season well. Cover and microwave 20 minutes; turn endives over halfway through.

Remove endives from casserole and discard ½ of cooking liquid.

Wrap endives in slices of ham and secure with toothpicks; replace in casserole. Pour in white sauce, season and top with cheese. Microwave 3 minutes uncovered.

Quick Vegetable Mix

(serves 4)

1 SERVING	182 CALORIES	22g CARBOHYDRATE
10g PROTEIN	8g FAT	3.0g FIBER

Setting: HIGH

Cooking Time: 24 minutes

Utensil: 12 cups (2.8 L) casserole with cover

1 tbsp	(15 ml) butter
1	medium onion, chopped
1	garlic clove, smashed and chopped
3	slices bacon, diced
1 lb	(500 g) fresh okra, ends snipped
4	tomatoes, peeled, seeded and chopped
1	green pepper, diced
1 tsp	(5 ml) chopped jalapeno pepper
1 tbsp	(15 ml) curry powder
1 tbsp	(15 ml) cumin powder
1 tsp	(5 ml) olive oil
	salt and pepper

Microwave butter 1 minute in casserole uncovered.

Add onion, garlic and bacon; cover and microwave 6 minutes.

Add okra and mix; microwave 2 minutes covered.

Stir in tomatoes, green pepper, jalapeno, seasonings and oil; cover and microwave 7 minutes.

Mix well; finish microwaving 8 minutes covered.

Sprinkle with cheese if desired.

Trim ends from fresh okra.

 **3** Microwave onion, garlic and bacon 6 minutes covered. Then, add okra and microwave 2 minutes.

An easy way to **2** peel fresh tomatoes is to blanch them in boiling water for 2 to 3 minutes. The skin should separate quite easily from the flesh.

 **4** Stir in tomatoes, green pepper, jalapeno, seasonings and oil; cover and microwave 7 minutes.

Spaghetti Squash

(serves 4)

1 SERVING	57 CALORIES	2g CARBOHYDRATE
1g PROTEIN	6g FAT	trace FIBER

Setting: HIGH
Cooking Time: 25 minutes
Utensil: none

1		spaghetti squash
2 tbsp	(30 ml) butter	
	salt and pepper	
	butter to taste	

Cut squash in half lengthwise; remove all seeds and hair-like fibers.

Divide butter between halves and season very generously. Wrap loosely in pierced plastic wrap and place in microwave.

Microwave 25 minutes.

Remove from oven, scoop out squash and place in bowl. Add more butter to taste and serve as garnish with ocean perch.

Creamy Cauliflower

(serves 4)

1 SERVING	213 CALORIES	17g CARBOHYDRATE
5g PROTEIN	11g FAT	2.0g FIBER

Setting: HIGH
Cooking Time: 9 minutes
Utensil: 12 cups (2.8 L) casserole with cover

1 tbsp	(15 ml) butter
1	small cauliflower, in flowerets
2	large potatoes, peeled, cooked and diced
1	cucumber, peeled, seeded and diced
2	garlic cloves, smashed and chopped
1 tbsp	(15 ml) chopped parsley
2 tbsp	(30 ml) chopped pimento
1 cup	(250 ml) hot light cream
	salt and pepper
	few drops lemon juice

Place butter and cauliflower in casserole; season with salt, pepper and lemon juice. Cover and microwave 5 minutes.

Add potatoes, cucumber, garlic, parsley and pimento; mix well. Continue microwaving 2 minutes covered.

Mix again and stir in cream; finish microwaving 2 minutes uncovered.

Layered Asparagus Dish

(serves 4)

1 SERVING	174 CALORIES	14g CARBOHYDRATE
16g PROTEIN	15g FAT	1.0g FIBER

Setting: HIGH
Cooking Time: 15 minutes
Utensil: 12 cups (2.8 L) casserole with cover

1 lb	(500 g) fresh asparagus, pared
½ cup	(125 ml) water
1 cup	(250 ml) tomato sauce, heated
1 cup	(250 ml) white sauce, heated
¼ tsp	(1 ml) nutmeg
1 cup	(250 ml) grated Gruyère cheese
	salt and pepper

Place asparagus and water in casserole. Season with salt, cover and microwave 6 minutes.

Using tongs bring asparagus at bottom of casserole towards top; replace cover and microwave 6 more minutes. (If asparagus are very large continue microwaving an extra minute.)

Discard liquid from casserole and remove half of asparagus.

Add half of each: tomato sauce, white sauce, nutmeg and cheese.

Cover with remaining asparagus and repeat above layers. Cover and microwave 3 minutes.

Broccoli and Asparagus

(serves 4)

1 SERVING	79 CALORIES	6g CARBOHYDRATE
3g PROTEIN	5g FAT	1.0g FIBER

Setting: HIGH

Cooking Time: 9 minutes

Utensil: 12 cups (2.8 L) casserole with cover

1	bunch fresh asparagus, tips only
1 tbsp	(15 ml) butter
1	head broccoli, in flowerets
1 tbsp	(15 ml) chopped fresh ginger
3 tbsp	(45 ml) toasted slivered almonds
	salt and pepper

Slice asparagus tips in half lengthwise. Cut each half into 2 pieces. Place in casserole with butter, salt and pepper. Cover and microwave 4 minutes.

Add broccoli, ginger and almonds; mix well. Cover and microwave 5 minutes.

Serve.

Almond Cake

(serves 10-12)

1 SERVING	298 CALORIES	35g CARBOHYDRATE
5g PROTEIN	16g FAT	trace FIBER

Setting: MEDIUM

Cooking Time: 19 minutes

Utensil: 12 cups (3 L) bundt mold

1⅔ cups	(400 ml) all-purpose flour
1 cup	(250 ml) granulated sugar
¼ cup	(50 ml) powdered almonds
1 tsp	(5 ml) baking soda
¼ tsp	(1 ml) salt
¼ tsp	(1 ml) nutmeg
1 cup	(250 ml) milk
½ cup	(125 ml) vegetable oil
1	egg
1 tsp	(5 ml) vanilla
¼ cup	(50 ml) slivered almonds
½ cup	(125 ml) crushed pineapple
2	egg whites, beaten stiff

Lightly oil bundt mold and set aside.

Sift flour, sugar, powdered almonds, baking soda, salt and nutmeg into bowl of mixer. Using whisk attachment, mix at low speed for 2 minutes.

Add milk, oil, whole egg and vanilla; beat 2 minutes or until well incorporated.

Add almonds and pineapple; blend 2 minutes at low speed.

Using spatula fold in stiff egg whites until thoroughly incorporated.

Pour batter into mold and rap bottom on counter to settle mixture. Microwave 19 minutes, rotating 4 times.

Let cake stand in mold to cool. When ready to serve, ice with your favorite frosting.

Sift flour, sugar, powdered almonds, baking soda, salt and nutmeg into bowl of mixer.

Using whisk attachment, mix at low speed for 2 minutes.

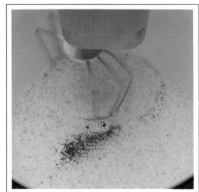

Beat milk, oil, egg and vanilla for 2 minutes or until well incorporated.

Add almonds and pineapple; blend 2 minutes at low speed.

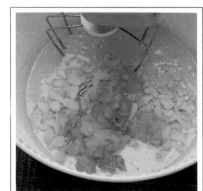

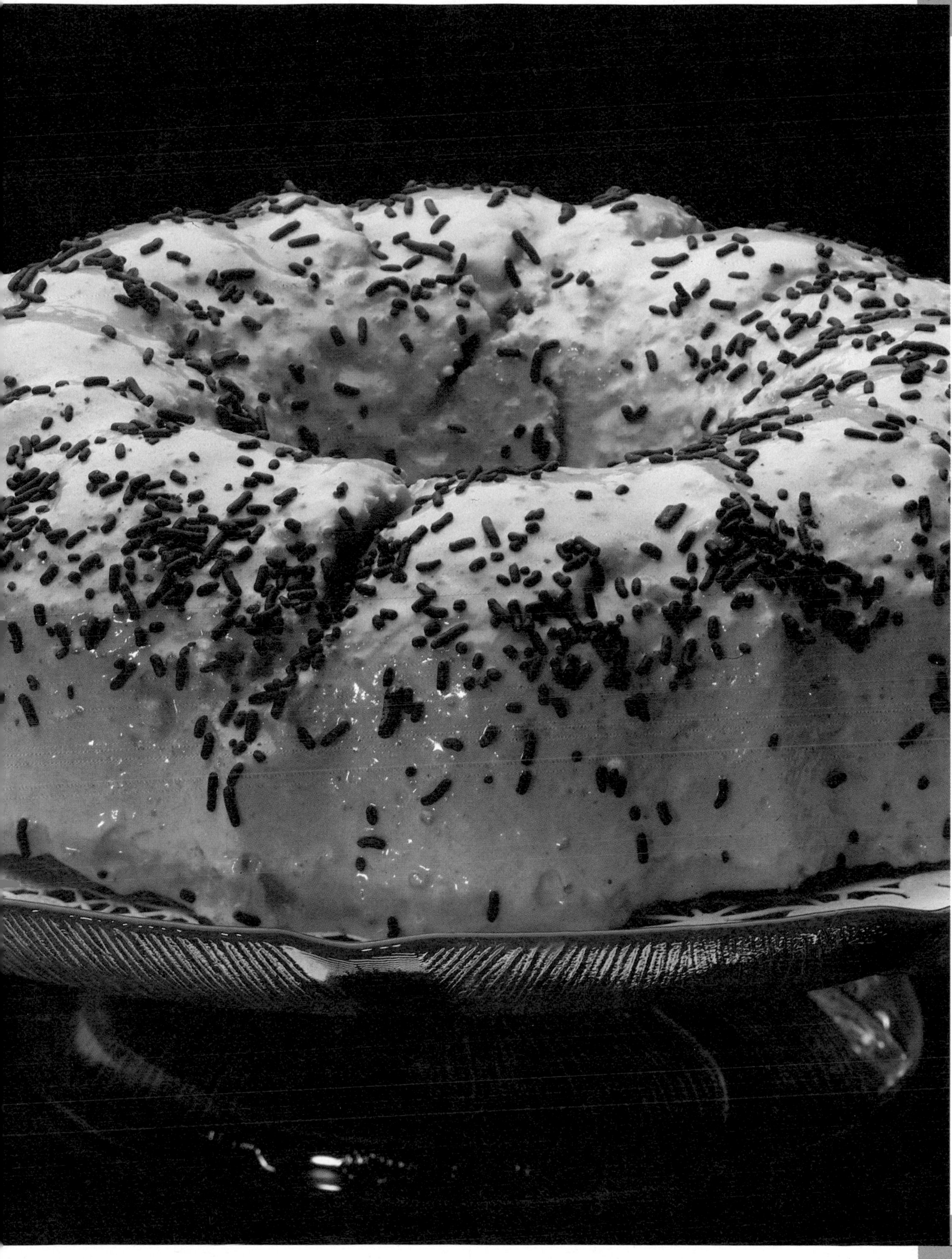

Almond Brownies

(serves 8)

1 SERVING	445 CALORIES	42g CARBOHYDRATE
8g PROTEIN	28g FAT	trace FIBER

Setting: HIGH

Cooking Time: 5½ minutes

Utensil: 8 cups (2 L) square plastic mold

½ cup	(125 ml) butter
¾ cup	(175 ml) granulated sugar
¼ cup	(50 ml) brown sugar
3	beaten eggs
1 tbsp	(15 ml) rum
4 tbsp	(60 ml) heavy cream
1 cup	(250 ml) sifted all-purpose flour
½ cup	(125 ml) cocoa
1 tsp	(5 ml) baking powder
1	egg white, beaten stiff
½ cup	(125 ml) slivered almonds

Grease plastic mold and set aside.

Place butter in glass bowl and microwave 1 minute uncovered or until melted.

Pour butter in large mixing bowl. Incorporate both sugars using electric hand beater.

Add beaten whole eggs, rum and cream; continue beating until well combined.

Sift dry ingredients into bowl; incorporate very well.

Using spatula fold in egg white and almonds. Pour batter into plastic mold and rap bottom on counter to settle mixture.

Microwave 4½ minutes uncovered. Rotate twice.

Remove from microwave and set aside to cool before serving.

Crepes Stuffed with Bananas

(serves 4)

1 SERVING	313 CALORIES	53g CARBOHYDRATE
6g PROTEIN	13g FAT	1.0g FIBER

Setting: MEDIUM-HIGH

Cooking Time: 4 minutes

Utensil: 8 cups (2 L) casserole

1 tbsp	(15 ml) butter
1 tbsp	(15 ml) maple syrup
4	bananas, sliced 1 in (2.5 cm) thick
2 tbsp	(30 ml) Caribbean Cream liqueur
3	egg whites
2 tbsp	(30 ml) granulated sugar
4	crepes
	juice 1½ oranges

Place butter and maple syrup in casserole; microwave 1 minute uncovered.

Add bananas, liqueur and orange juice; mix and microwave 3 minutes uncovered.

Meanwhile, beat egg whites until stiff. Add sugar slowly and continue beating 1 minute.

Spread banana mixture on crepes, roll and place on platter. Top with dollops of meringue and brown in conventional oven set at broil.

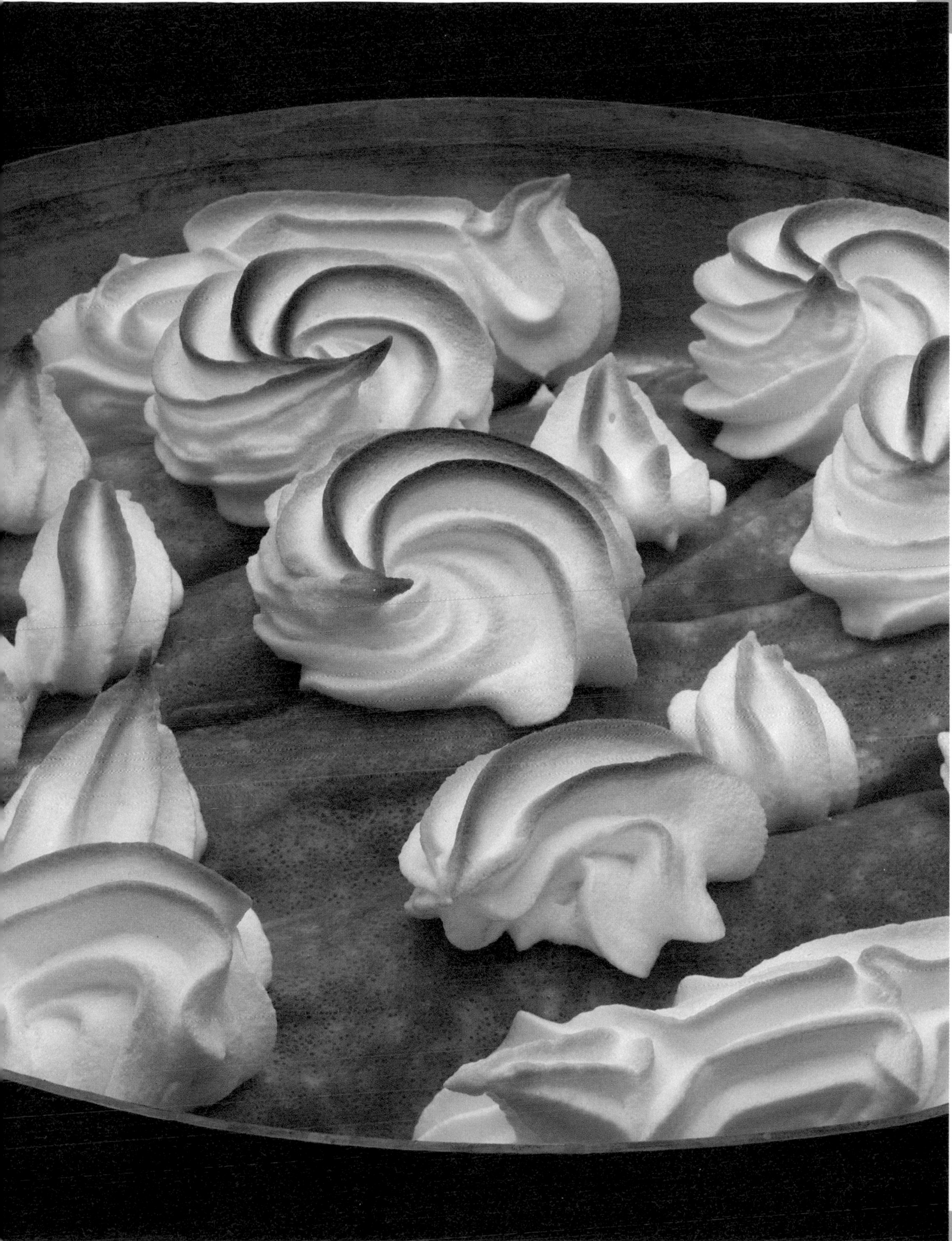

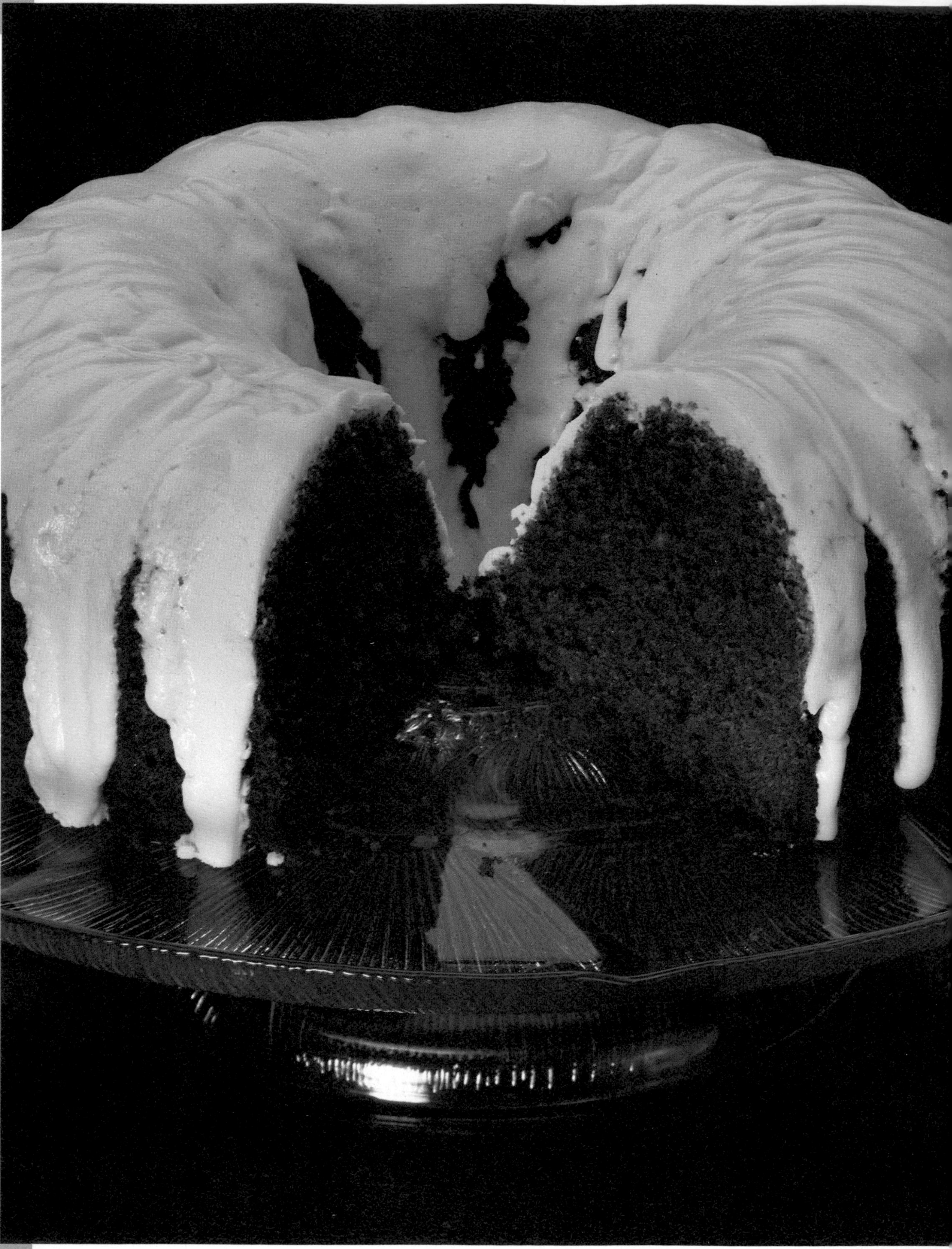

Chocolate Cake

(serves 10-12)

1 SERVING	396 CALORIES	38g CARBOHYDRATE
6g PROTEIN	24g FAT	trace FIBER

Setting: MEDIUM

Cooking Time: 29 minutes

Utensil: 12 cups (3 L) bundt mold

1 cup	(250 ml) granulated sugar
1½ cups	(375 ml) all-purpose flour
½ cup	(125 ml) cocoa
1½ tbsp	(25 ml) baking powder
¼ tsp	(1 ml) salt
¼ cup	(50 ml) powdered almonds
1 cup	(250 ml) soft unsalted butter
1 cup	(250 ml) milk
2 tbsp	(30 ml) Tia Maria
2	egg yolks
2	whole eggs
3	egg whites, beaten stiff
	oil

Lightly oil bundt mold and set aside.

Sift granulated sugar, flour, cocoa, baking powder, salt and powdered almonds into bowl of mixer. Using dough hook, mix at low speed for 2 minutes.

Add butter to bowl; continue mixing at medium speed until well incorporated. If necessary use spatula occasionally to prevent mixture from riding up sides.

Reduce mixer speed to low. Add milk and Tia Maria; blend for 1 minute.

Replace dough hook with whisk attachment. Increase speed to medium and add yolks and whole eggs; beat about 4 to 5 minutes.

Using spatula, fold in stiff egg whites until thoroughly incorporated.

Pour batter into mold and rap bottom on counter to settle mixture. Microwave 29 minutes, rotating 4 times.

Let cake stand in mold to cool. When ready to serve, ice with your favorite frosting.

Tasty Strawberry Sauce

1 RECIPE	800 CALORIES	187g CARBOHYDRATE
7g PROTEIN	.5g FAT	2.5g FIBER

Setting: HIGH

Cooking Time: 7 minutes

Utensil: 8 cups (2 L) casserole

15 oz	(425 g) package frozen strawberries
4 tbsp	(60 ml) black currant jelly
2 tbsp	(30 ml) orange liqueur
2 tbsp	(30 ml) cornstarch
4 tbsp	(60 ml) cold water

Thaw strawberries according to directions on package.

Place strawberries, jelly and liqueur in casserole. Microwave 4 minutes uncovered.

Mix cornstarch with water; stir into sauce and continue microwaving 3 minutes.

Cool and pour over ice cream or drizzle over sponge cake.

Rhubarb Sauce

1 RECIPE	1661 CALORIES	344g CARBOHYDRATE
4g PROTEIN	27g FAT	trace FIBER

Setting: HIGH

Cooking Time: 31 minutes

Utensil: 12 cups (2.8 L) casserole with cover

4 cups	(1 L) frozen rhubarb
3 tbsp	(45 ml) light rum
1 cup	(250 ml) granulated sugar
½ cup	(125 ml) brown sugar
¼ cup	(50 ml) freshly squeezed orange juice
2 tbsp	(30 ml) butter
2 tbsp	(30 ml) cornstarch
5 tbsp	(75 ml) cold water
	chopped rind 1 lemon
	chopped rind 1 orange

Place rhubarb in casserole and pour in rum.

Add both sugars, orange juice, butter and chopped rinds.

Mix slightly and cover; microwave 30 minutes.

Mix rhubarb sauce well. Mix cornstarch with water; stir into sauce. Microwave 1 minute uncovered.

Serve with cake or over ice cream.

It is not **1** necessary to defrost the rhubarb before microwaving.

Place rhubarb in **2** casserole and pour in rum.

3 Add both sugars

4 Add orange juice, butter and chopped rinds.

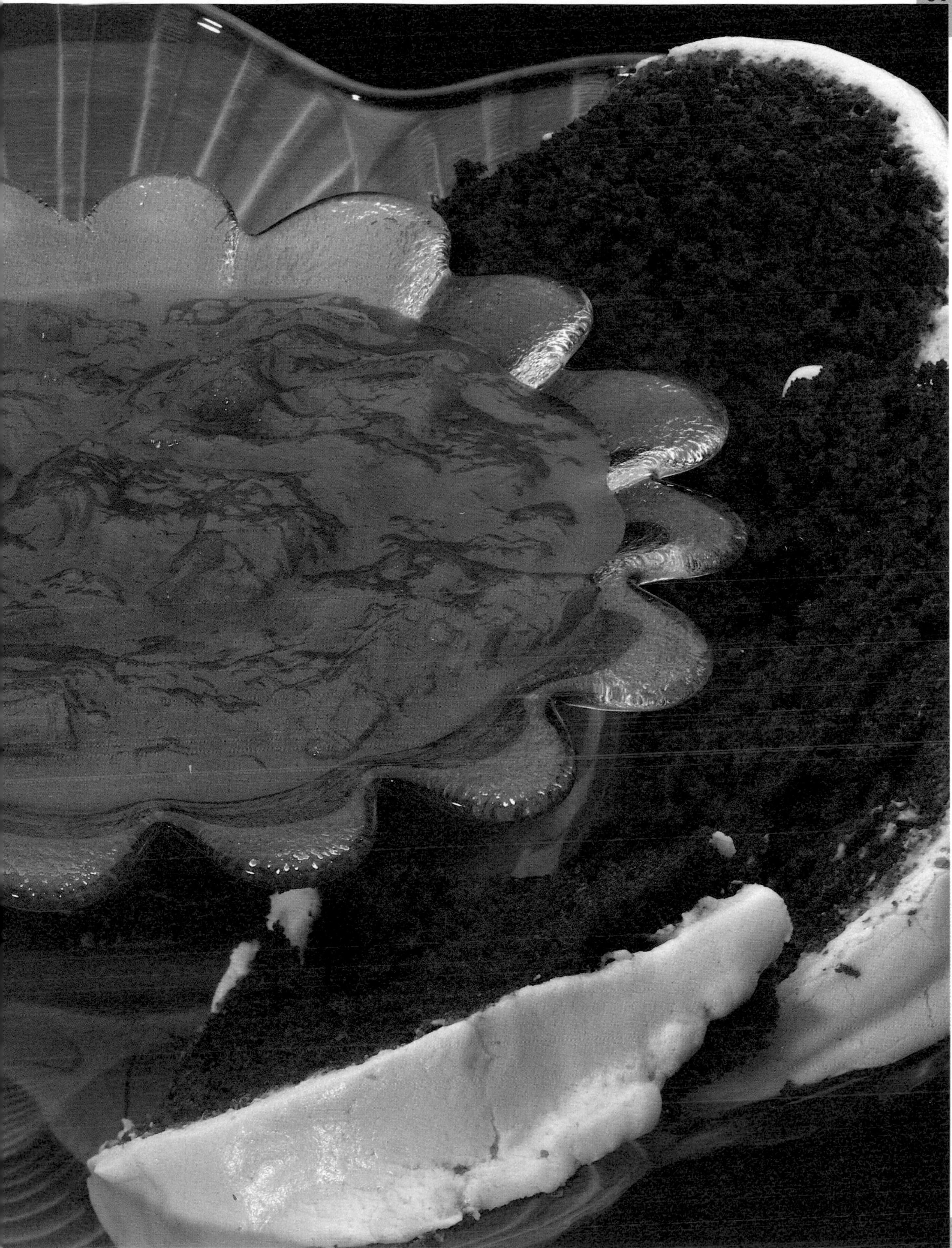

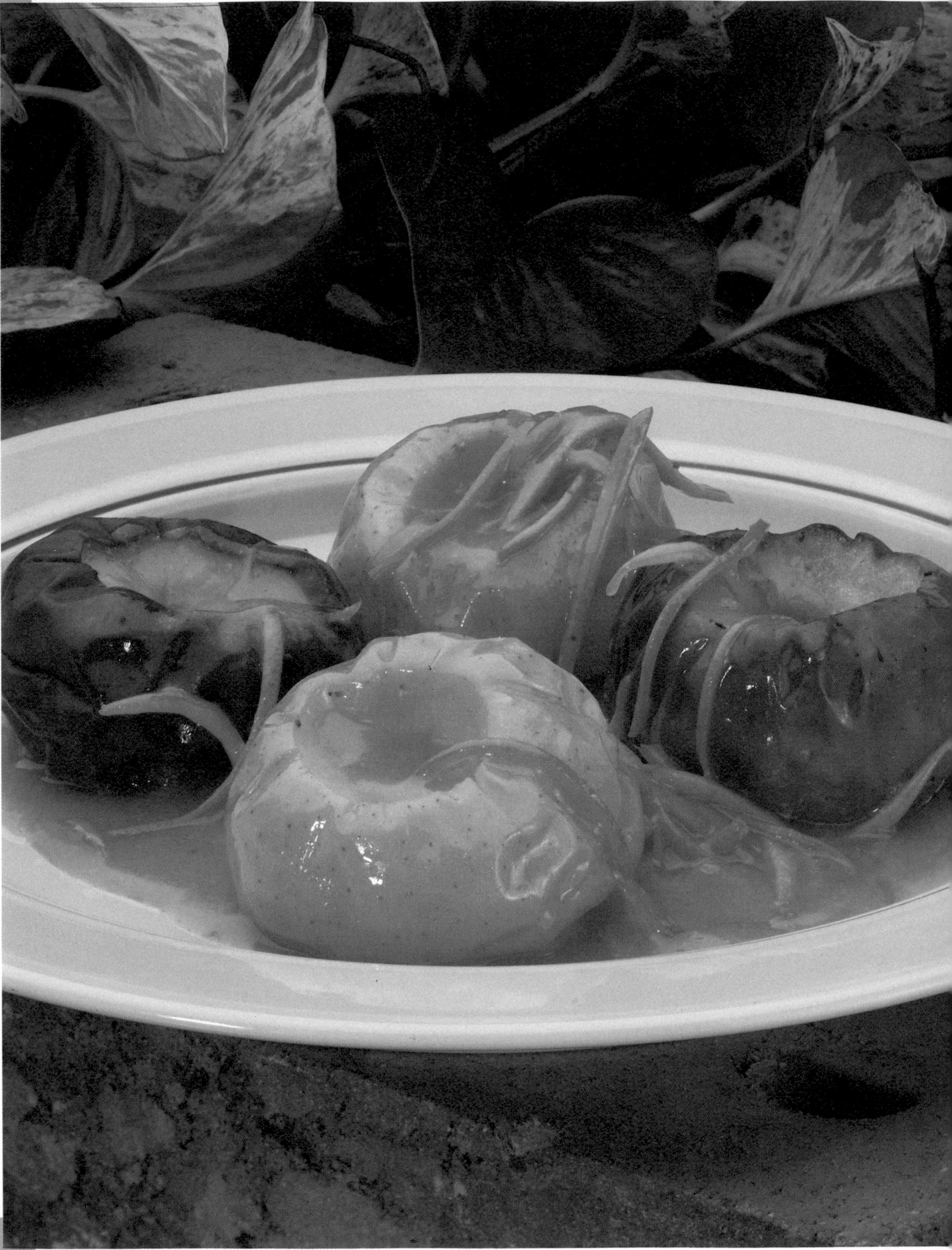

Baked Apples

(serves 4)

1 SERVING	298 CALORIES	39g CARBOHYDRATE
1g PROTEIN	10g FAT	1.0g FIBER

Setting: HIGH

Cooking Time: 12 minutes

Utensil: 8 cups (2 L) casserole with cover

4	large baking apples
3 tbsp	(45 ml) brown sugar
2 tbsp	(30 ml) butter
2 tbsp	(30 ml) heavy cream
¼ tsp	(1 ml) nutmeg
½ cup	(125 ml) light rum
1 tbsp	(15 ml) cornstarch
2 tbsp	(30 ml) cold water
	rind 1 orange in julienne

Core apples and using small knife score around middle. This will prevent skin from cracking during cooking.

Cut away a bit of apple flesh at one end to make hole wider for filling. Place apples in casserole.

Mix brown sugar with butter in small bowl. Stir in cream and nutmeg.

Pour rum into bottom of casserole and fill apple cavities with cream mixture.

Cover and microwave 11 minutes.

Remove apples from casserole and set aside.

Add orange rind to juices in casserole. Mix cornstarch with water; stir into sauce to thicken. Microwave 1 minute uncovered.

Pour sauce over apples and serve.

Core apples. **1**

3 Cut away a bit of apple flesh at one end to make hole wider for filling. Place apples in casserole and pour in rum.

2 Using small knife score apples around middle to prevent skin from cracking during cooking.

4 Fill apple cavities with cream mixture.

Dessert Drink

(serves 4)

1 SERVING	248 CALORIES	19g CARBOHYDRATE
1g PROTEIN	17g FAT	trace FIBER

Setting: HIGH
Cooking Time: 2 minutes
Utensil: 12 cups (2.8 L) casserole

4	lemon slices
3	cinnamon sticks
1 tbsp	(15 ml) grated orange rind
2	cloves
3 tbsp	(45 ml) dark rum
3 tbsp	(45 ml) brown sugar
1 tbsp	(15 ml) honey
4 cups	(1 L) strong black coffee, hot
¾ cup	(175 ml) heavy cream, whipped
	granulated sugar
	dash cinnamon

Coat rims of 4 tall-stemmed glasses with lemon. Dip in granulated sugar and set aside.

Place remaining ingredients, except cream and cinnamon, in casserole. Microwave 2 minutes uncovered.

Pour into glasses and top with dollops of whipped cream. Sprinkle with dash of cinnamon and serve immediately.

Creamy Rice Pudding

(serves 4-6)

1 SERVING	345 CALORIES	53g CARBOHYDRATE
9g PROTEIN	7g FAT	1.0g FIBER

Setting: MEDIUM-HIGH and LOW
Cooking Time: 39 minutes
Utensil: 12 cups (2.8 L) casserole with cover

1 cup	(250 ml) long grain rice, rinsed
½ cup	(125 ml) brown sugar
3½ cups	(875 ml) hot milk
1 tbsp	(15 ml) grated lemon rind
¼ cup	(50 ml) sultana raisins
½ cup	(125 ml) light cream
2 tbsp	(30 ml) mixed candied fruit
1 tbsp	(15 ml) cinnamon
1	beaten egg

Place rice in casserole and sprinkle in sugar. Mix in milk and lemon rind. Cover and microwave 18 minutes at MEDIUM-HIGH, stirring twice.

Add raisins, cream, fruit and cinnamon; incorporate well. Continue microwaving 19 minutes covered, stirring occasionally.

Add egg, mix well and finish microwaving 2 minutes at LOW uncovered.

Serve plain or drizzled with maple syrup.

Creamy Cheesecake

(serves 8-10)

1 SERVING	403 CALORIES	28g CARBOHYDRATE
7g PROTEIN	30g FAT	--g FIBER

Setting: HIGH

Cooking Time: 8¾ minutes

Utensil: 6 cups (1.5 L) glass pie plate

¾ cup	(175 ml) crushed chocolate wafers
¼ cup	(50 ml) fine granulated sugar
¼ cup	(50 ml) soft butter
2	8 oz (227 g) packages cream cheese, soft
½ cup	(125 ml) fine granulated sugar
3 tbsp	(45 ml) orange liqueur
1 tbsp	(15 ml) grated lemon rind
1 tbsp	(15 ml) grated orange rind
1 tbsp	(15 ml) cornstarch
3	large eggs
½ cup	(125 ml) heavy cream, whipped
1	egg white, beaten stiff

First, prepare crust by combining wafers, ¼ cup (50 ml) sugar and butter until thoroughly blended. Press into pie plate and microwave ¾ minute uncovered. Set aside to cool while filling is being prepared.

Place cheese and second measure of sugar in bowl of mixer; blend until smooth.

Add liqueur, rinds and cornstarch; mix to incorporate.

Add eggs one at a time, mixing well between additions.

Fold in whipped cream and egg white with spatula.

Pour filling into cooled crust and smooth with spatula. Microwave 8 minutes uncovered. Rotate every 2 minutes.

Remove from microwave and set aside to cool. Refrigerate 2 hours before serving.

MICROWAVE II

Microwave:

Microwave II is the sequel to the first microwave cookbook in the Smart & Simple series. It is designed to pick up where the first book left off with brand new recipes and ideas based on what you have already learned and practiced. By now you are probably at ease with this new style of cooking and are well aware of what this tool can do to accommodate your needs and your family's. Isn't it just remarkable how versatile and easy microwave cooking can be once you have a little experience? The old saying 'practice makes perfect' certainly rings true. I am sure you can see the difference in your meals and we can certainly confirm that our recipes are becoming more and more inventive and interesting!

Not to spend too much time on what you already know, here are a few reminders for successful microwave cooking:

— position the thickest end of irregularly-shaped foods (chicken legs, for example) toward the walls of the microwave.

— stir foods by moving them from the outside-in to help even cooking.

— invest in a selection of 'microwave-proof' utensils for everyday use.

— when using a browning grill, always read the manufacturer's instructions for possible differences in preheating times and microwave settings.

— take several minutes to read the recipe, from start to finish, before your start.

— and above all, have fun!

All our recipes were tested in a 650-watt oven with power settings equivalent to the ones on the chart below. Because microwave ovens differ in terms of their maximum power and therefore, power settings, study the chart before beginning any recipe.

Setting	Approximate wattage	Percent of power
HIGH	650	100
MEDIUM-HIGH	485	75
MEDIUM	325	50
LOW	160	25

Please consult your manufacturer's guide booklet for any adjustments regarding settings that might be needed.

Shrimp Spread

(serves 6 to 8)

SERVING	186 CALORIES	16g CARBOHYDRATE
g PROTEIN	10g FAT	1.5g FIBER

Setting: HIGH

Cooking time: 3 minutes

Utensil: 12 cups (3 L) casserole

oz	(113 g) can medium shrimp, drained and chopped
cup	(125 ml) pitted black olives
cup	(50 ml) chopped onion
tsp	(5 ml) chopped fresh parsley
⅓ lb	(150 g) grated cheddar cheese
	dash hot pepper sauce
	toasted baguette slices

Place shrimp in casserole. Pat olives dry and chop; add to casserole along with remaining ingredients, except bread.

Microwave 3 minutes uncovered, stirring occasionally.

Mix well and spoon onto toasted baguette slices. Serve with a selection of fresh cheeses.

Oyster Nibbles

(serves 4 to 6)

1 SERVING	121 CALORIES	12g CARBOHYDRATE
7g PROTEIN	5g FAT	0.7g FIBER

Setting: HIGH and MEDIUM

Cooking time: 2½ minutes

Utensil: 12 cups (3 L) casserole

1½ tbsp	(25 ml) butter
¼ cup	(50 ml) Folonari Chardonnay white wine
¼ cup	(50 ml) water
1 tsp	(5 ml) chopped fresh parsley
18	shucked oysters
	salt and freshly ground pepper
	lemon juice to taste

Place butter, wine, water and parsley in casserole. Season and microwave 2 minutes uncovered at HIGH.

Add oysters and lemon juice; microwave 30 seconds uncovered at MEDIUM.

Let stand 1 minute, drain and serve oysters with toast.

Spinach Chicken Muffins

(serves 4)

1 SERVING	645 CALORIES	44g CARBOHYDRATE
35g PROTEIN	37g FAT	1.9g FIBER

Setting: HIGH and MEDIUM
Cooking time: 21 minutes
Utensil: 8 cups (2 L) rectangular dish
12 cups (3 L) casserole

4	English muffins, split in half
2 tbsp	(30 ml) butter
1	whole chicken breast, skinned, deboned and split into two
½ lb	(250 g) fresh mushrooms, cleaned and diced
1 cup	(250 ml) cooked chopped spinach
2 cups	(500 ml) hot white sauce
½ cup	(125 ml) grated mozzarella cheese
¼ tsp	(1 ml) nutmeg
1 tbsp	(15 ml) chopped fresh parsley
	salt and pepper

Place English muffins in rectangular dish and set aside.

Place butter in casserole and microwave 1 minute uncovered at HIGH.

Add chicken and season; cover and microwave 8 minutes at MEDIUM.

Turn chicken over; cover and continue microwaving 7 minutes.

Remove chicken from casserole and set aside. When cool, dice meat.

Place mushrooms in casserole and season well. Cover and microwave 3 minutes at HIGH.

Transfer mushrooms to bowl. Add diced chicken, spinach, white sauce and cheese; mix very well.

Sprinkle in nutmeg and parsley; correct seasoning.

Pour over muffins and microwave 2 minutes uncovered at HIGH.

Mini Pita Bites

(serves 4 to 6)

1 SERVING	219 CALORIES	29g CARBOHYDRATE
12g PROTEIN	6g FAT	0.5g FIBER

Setting: HIGH
Cooking time: 2 minutes
Utensil: large microwave serving platter

½ cup	(125 ml) finely chopped ham
1 cup	(250 ml) ricotta cheese
¼ cup	(50 ml) chopped sweet pimento
1	garlic clove, smashed and finely chopped
1 tsp	(5 ml) chopped fresh parsley
12-18	mini pita breads
	few drops lemon juice
	salt and pepper

Place all ingredients, except pita breads, in food processor. Blend until puréed.

Cut off one corner of each pita bread and fill with stuffing. Place on serving platter and microwave 2 minutes uncovered.

Serve with an assortment of cheese and condiments if desired.

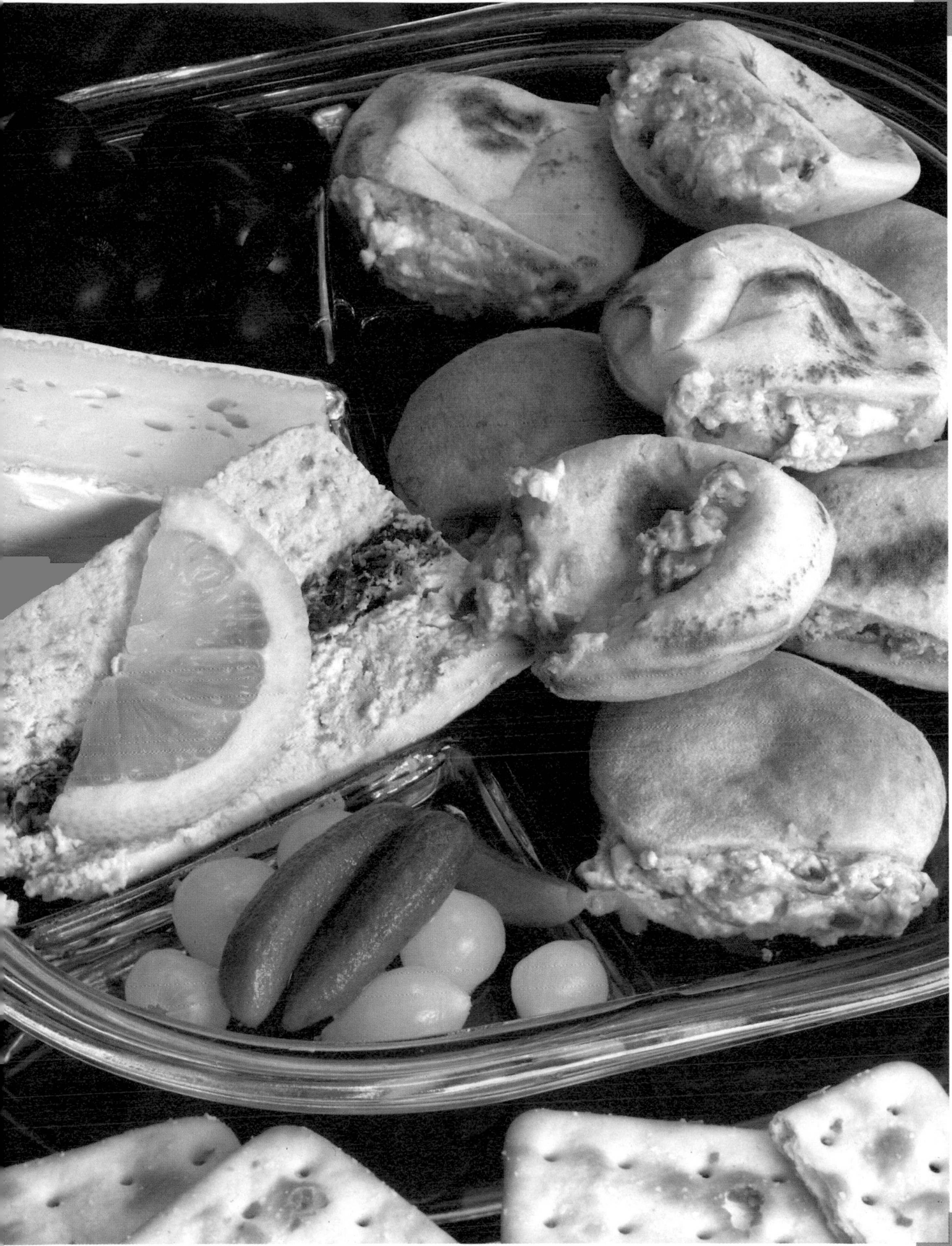

Egg and Vegetable Scramble

(serves 2)

1 SERVING	269 CALORIES	18g CARBOHYDRATE
16g PROTEIN	15g FAT	1.2g FIBER

Setting: HIGH and MEDIUM-HIGH

Cooking time: 5 minutes 10 seconds

Utensil: 12 cups (3 L) casserole

1 tsp	(5 ml) butter
½	yellow pepper, diced
3	eggs
¼ cup	(50 ml) grated Gruyère cheese
	salt and pepper
	few drops Tabasco sauce
	several slices toasted bread

Place butter and yellow pepper in casserole. Season, cover and microwave 2 minutes at HIGH.

Beat eggs, season and add Tabasco; mix again. Pour into casserole and mix well; microwave 1 minute uncovered at HIGH.

Whisk well; continue microwaving 1 minute 10 seconds.

Spoon scrambled eggs on toast, top with cheese and microwave 1 minute uncovered at MEDIUM-HIGH.

Eggplant Dip

(serves 6 to 8)

1 SERVING	33 CALORIES	4g CARBOHYDRATE
0g PROTEIN	2g FAT	0.7g FIBER

Setting: HIGH

Cooking time: 15 minutes

Utensil: trivet

1	large eggplant
1 tsp	(5 ml) vegetable oil
1	tomato, finely chopped
1	garlic clove, smashed and chopped
1 tsp	(5 ml) chopped fresh parsley
1 tbsp	(15 ml) olive oil
	dash hot pepper sauce
	salt and pepper

Slice eggplant in half lengthwise. Score flesh deeply both crosswise and lengthwise. Brush with vegetable oil and place halves on trivet; microwave 15 minutes uncovered.

Scoop out cooked flesh and place in food processor. Add remaining ingredients and blend until thoroughly incorporated and smooth.

Serve dip with crackers and assorted fresh vegetables.

 Score flesh **1** deeply both crosswise and lengthwise.

3 Scoop out cooked eggplant flesh.

Brush with **2** vegetable oil and place on trivet; microwave 15 minutes uncovered.

 **4** Place in food processor and add remaining ingredients. Purée.

Shrimp and Tuna Combo

(serves 4)

1 SERVING	314 CALORIES	9g CARBOHYDRATE
27g PROTEIN	19g FAT	1.3g FIBER

Setting: HIGH

Cooking time: 4 minutes

Utensil:	12 cups (3 L) casserole
1 lb	(500 g) medium shrimp
7 oz	(198 g) can tuna in oil, well drained and flaked
½	celery stalk, thinly sliced
12	cherry tomatoes, halved
12	water chestnuts
½ cup	(125 ml) vinaigrette
¼ tsp	(1 ml) tarragon
	juice ½ lemon
	salt and pepper
	lettuce leaves

Place shrimp in casserole and pour in enough hot water to cover. Add lemon juice and cover with plastic wrap; microwave 3 minutes.

Stir well, moving shrimps near outside of casserole towards centre. Replace cover and microwave 1 minute.

Remove casserole from microwave and let stand 4 to 5 minutes.

Cool under cold water, peel and devein shrimp.

Place shrimp in bowl with all other ingredients; marinate 1 hour and serve on lettuce leaves.

Rigatoni and Polish Sausage

(serves 3)

1 SERVING	488 CALORIES	40g CARBOHYDRATE
22g PROTEIN	27g FAT	2.7g FIBER

Setting: HIGH

Cooking time: 7 minutes

Utensil:	12 cups (3 L) casserole
½ lb	(250 g) Polish sausage links, sliced thick
1 tbsp	(15 ml) butter
4	thick slices yellow squash, quartered
½	green pepper, thinly sliced
5	cherry tomatoes, halved
½ cup	(125 ml) hot chicken stock
2 tbsp	(30 ml) cornstarch
3 tbsp	(45 ml) cold water
2	portions hot cooked rigatoni
½ cup	(125 ml) grated mozzarella cheese
	salt and pepper

If not already done, remove casing from sausage slices; set sausage aside.

Place butter, squash and green pepper in casserole; cover and microwave 4 minutes.

Season and add tomatoes, sausage slices and chicken stock; microwave 1 minute uncovered.

Mix cornstarch with water; stir into sauce. Add pasta, mix well and add cheese. Mix, microwave 2 minutes uncovered and serve.

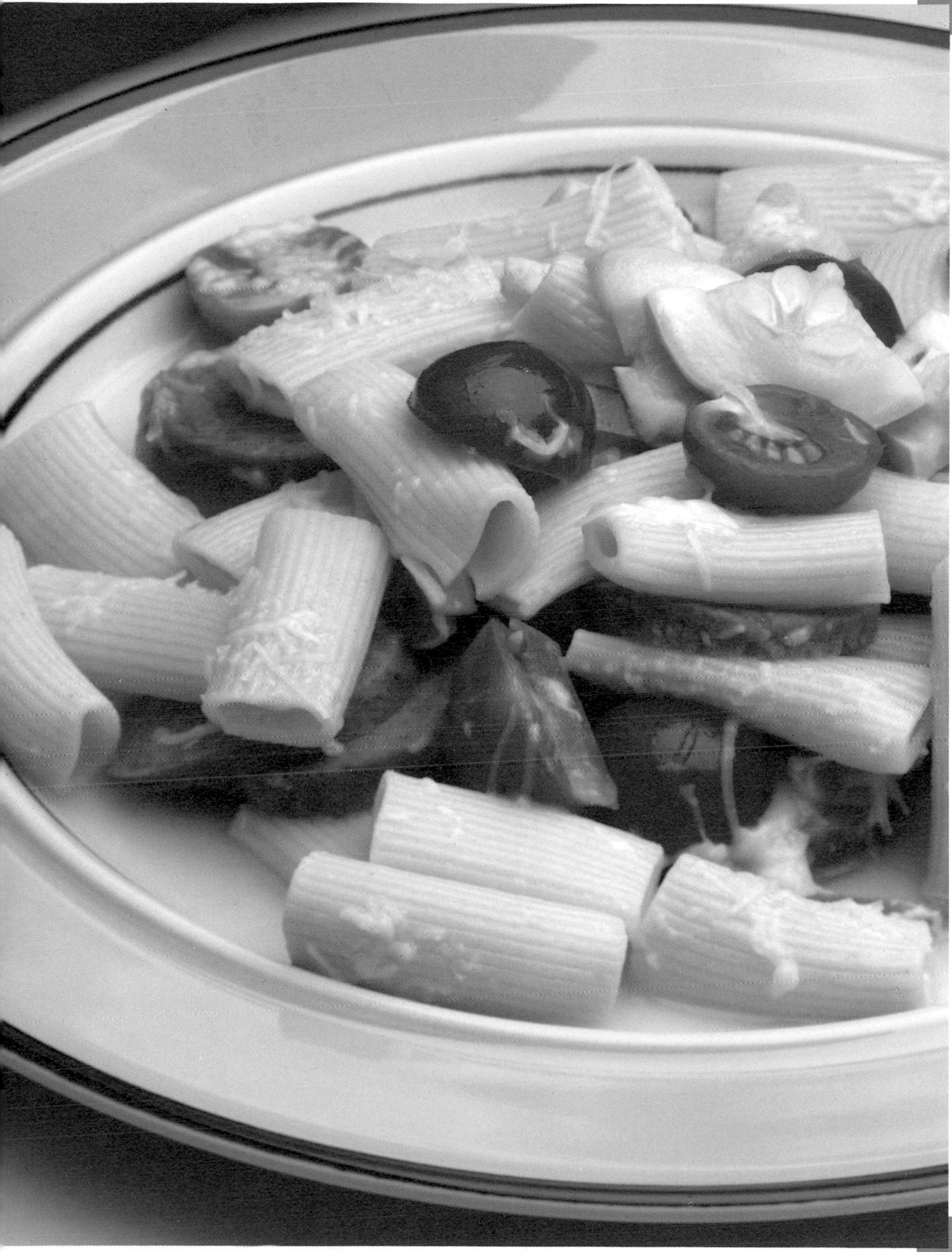

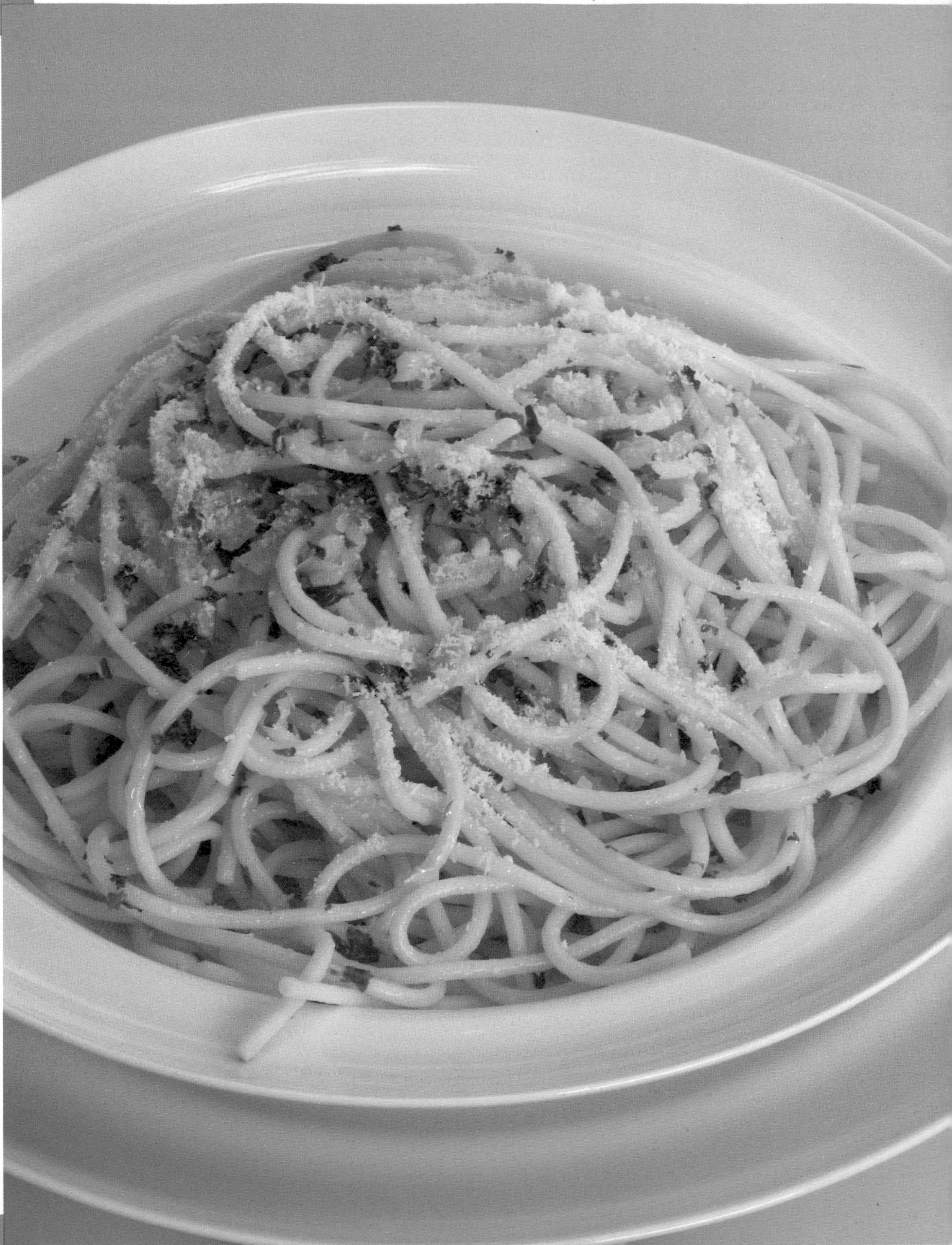

Spaghetti Provençale

(serves 2)

1 SERVING	286 CALORIES	36g CARBOHYDRATE
5g PROTEIN	13g FAT	1.4g FIBER

Setting: HIGH
Cooking time: 2 minutes
Utensil: 12 cups (3 L) casserole

	garlic clove, smashed and chopped
2 tbsp	(30 ml) chopped fresh parsley
	large shallots, chopped
2 tbsp	(30 ml) butter
	portions hot cooked spaghetti
2 tbsp	(30 ml) grated Parmesan cheese
	salt and white pepper

Place garlic, parsley, shallots and butter in casserole. Microwave 1 minute uncovered.

Stir and add spaghetti; season well. Microwave 1 minute uncovered.

Mix in cheese and serve immediately.

Spaghetti à la Valpolicella

(serves 2)

1 SERVING	436 CALORIES	51g CARBOHYDRATE
13g PROTEIN	20g FAT	2.5g FIBER

Setting: HIGH and MEDIUM
Cooking time: 10 minutes
Utensil: 12 cups (3 L) casserole

2 tbsp	(30 ml) olive oil
1	onion, finely chopped
½ lb	(250 g) fresh mushrooms, cleaned and halved
¼ cup	(50 ml) Folonari Valpolicella red wine
1¼ cups	(300 ml) hot brown sauce
1 tsp	(5 ml) chopped fresh parsley
2	portions hot cooked spaghetti
	salt and pepper
	grated Parmesan or other cheese

Place oil, onion and mushrooms in casserole. Cover and microwave 3 minutes at HIGH.

Add wine and brown sauce; mix well. Sprinkle in parsley, season and microwave 5 minutes uncovered at HIGH.

Stir in spaghetti and microwave 2 minutes uncovered at MEDIUM.

Serve with grated cheese.

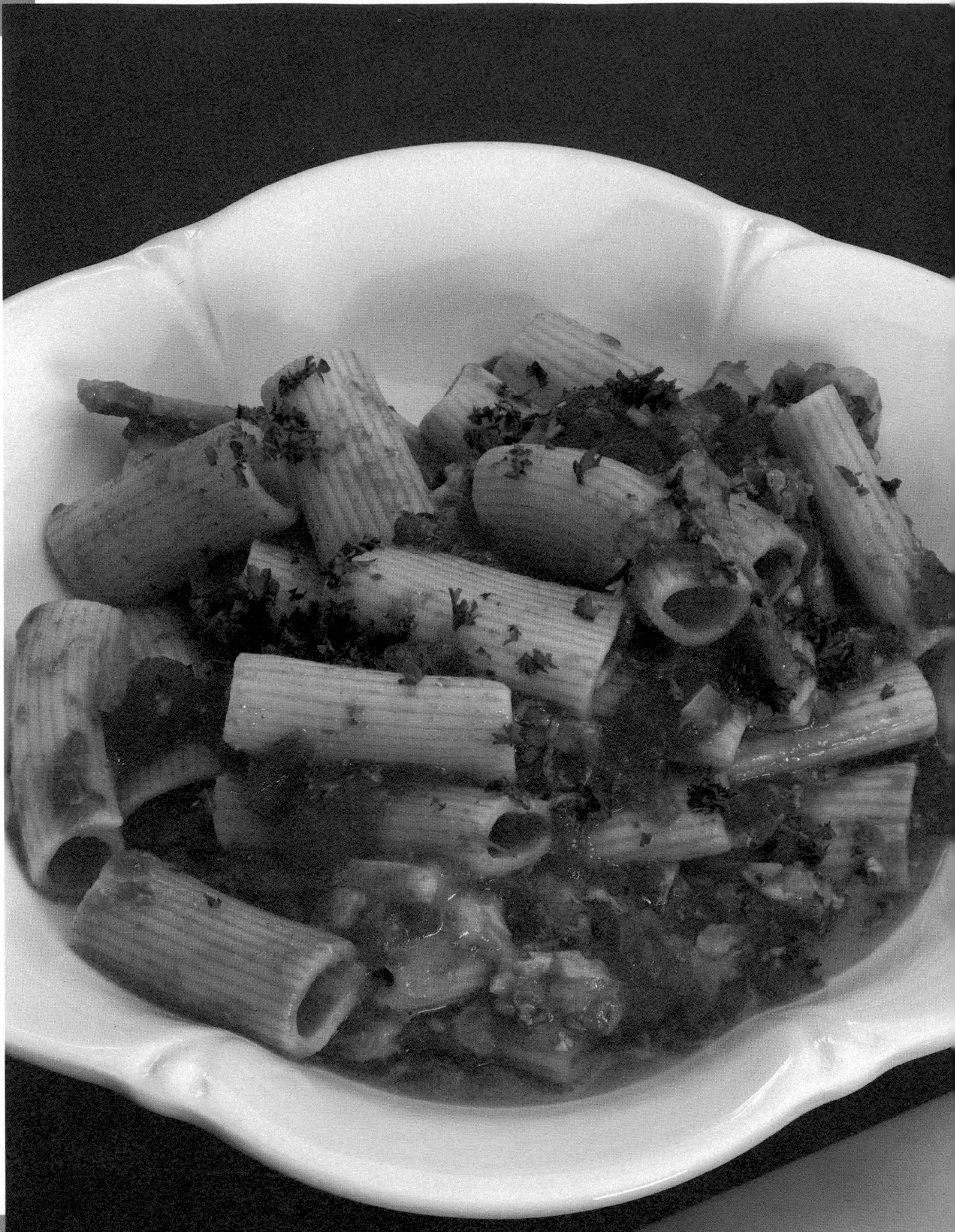

Greek Pasta Dinner

(serves 3)

1 SERVING	369 CALORIES	50g CARBOHYDRATE
15g PROTEIN	12g FAT	2.6g FIBER

Setting: HIGH

Cooking time: 16 minutes

Utensil: 12 cups (3 L) casserole

1	garlic clove, smashed and chopped
½	onion, chopped
½	green pepper, chopped
1 tbsp	(15 ml) oil
2	slices back bacon, in julienne
2 oz	(60 g) feta cheese, cut up
28 oz	(796 ml) can tomatoes, drained and chopped
3 tbsp	(45 ml) tomato paste
3	portions hot cooked rigatoni
	few crushed chillies
	dash paprika
	salt and pepper

Place garlic, onion, green pepper and oil in casserole. Cover and microwave 3 minutes.

Add bacon, cheese and crushed chillies; microwave 3 minutes, covered.

Add tomatoes; season well with paprika, salt and pepper. Stir in tomato paste, cover and microwave 7 minutes.

Add pasta, correct seasoning and microwave 3 minutes uncovered.

Place garlic, onion, green pepper and oil in casserole. Cover and microwave 3 minutes.

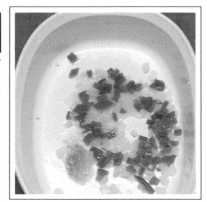

Add tomatoes; season well with paprika, salt and pepper.

Add bacon, cheese and crushed chillies; microwave 3 minutes, covered.

Stir in tomato paste, cover and microwave 7 minutes.

Green Lasagne

(serves 6 to 8)

1 SERVING	800 CALORIES	67g CARBOHYDRATE
35g PROTEIN	44g FAT	3.1g FIBER

Setting: HIGH

Cooking time: 56 minutes

Utensil: 12 cups (3 L) casserole
8 cups (2 L) rectangular dish

1	head cauliflower, in flowerets
2	heads broccoli, in flowerets
2 cups	(500 ml) hot chicken stock
1	yellow pepper, thinly sliced
½	zucchini, diced large
¾	1 lb (500 g) package spinach lasagne noodles, cooked, well drained and cooled
½ lb	(250 g) ricotta cheese
2 cups	(500 ml) finely grated Gruyère cheese
3 cups	(750 ml) hot white sauce
	paprika to taste
	salt and pepper

Place cauliflower and broccoli in casserole with chicken stock. Cover and microwave 4 minutes.

Stir well; continue microwaving 4 minutes.

Remove vegetables from casserole using slotted spoon, chop and set aside.

Leaving chicken stock in casserole, add yellow pepper and zucchini; cover and microwave 3 minutes. Drain vegetables and set aside.

Begin layering buttered rectangular dish with lasagne noodles to completely cover bottom. It is best that they overlap slightly.

Add half of chopped vegetables, half of ricotta, one-third of Gruyère and paprika to taste.

Add half of yellow pepper and zucchini, one-third of white sauce, season and start layering all over again with noodles.

End with noodles, followed by layer of white sauce and grated Gruyère cheese.

Cover with plastic wrap and microwave 30 minutes.

Rotate dish; continue microwaving 15 minutes.

Let stand 5 minutes before serving.

Begin layering buttered dish with lasagne noodles to completely cover bottom.

Add half of chopped vegetables.

Add half of ricotta, one-third of Gruyère and paprika to taste.

Add half of yellow pepper and zucchini, one-third of white sauce, season and start layering all over again beginning with noodles.

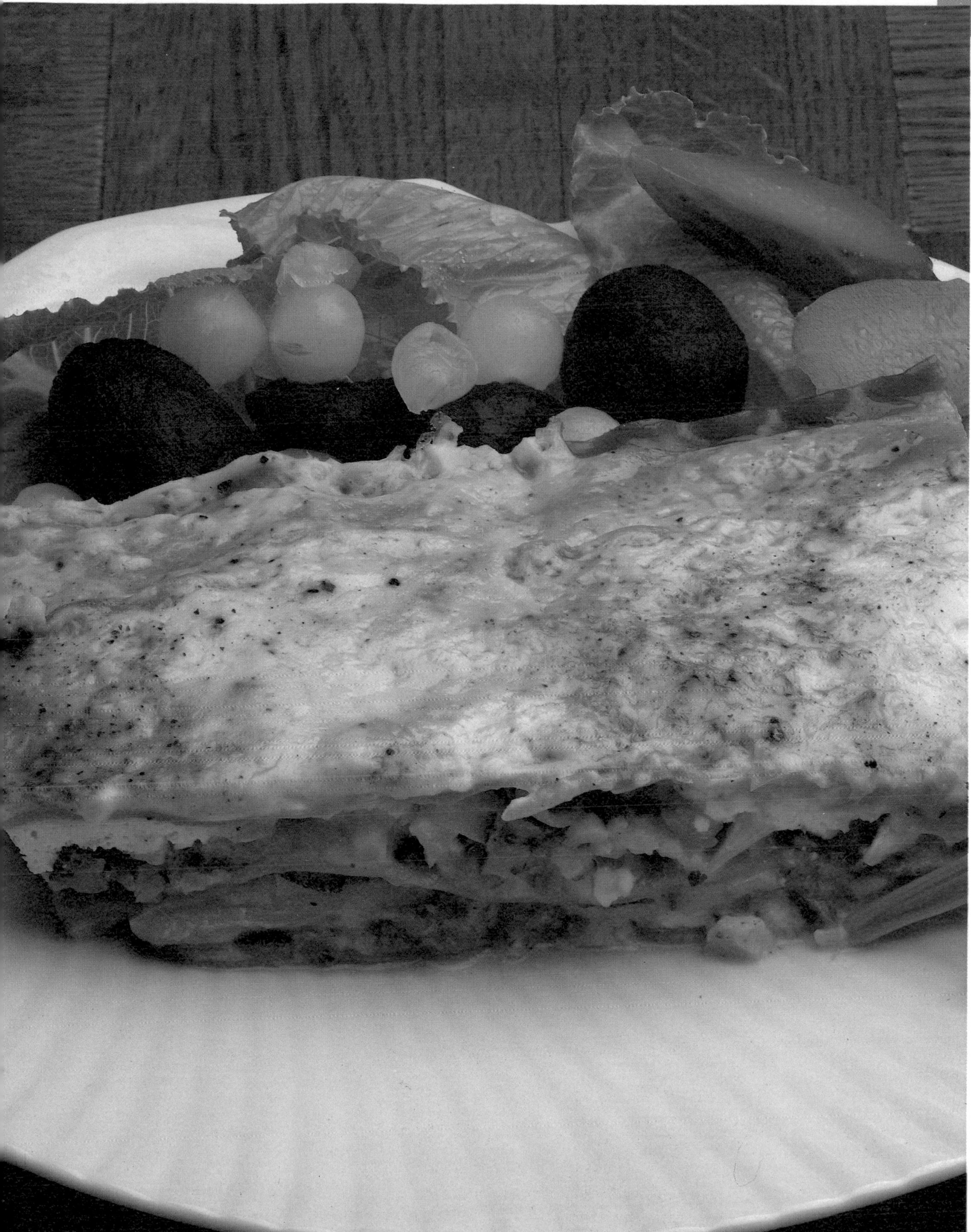

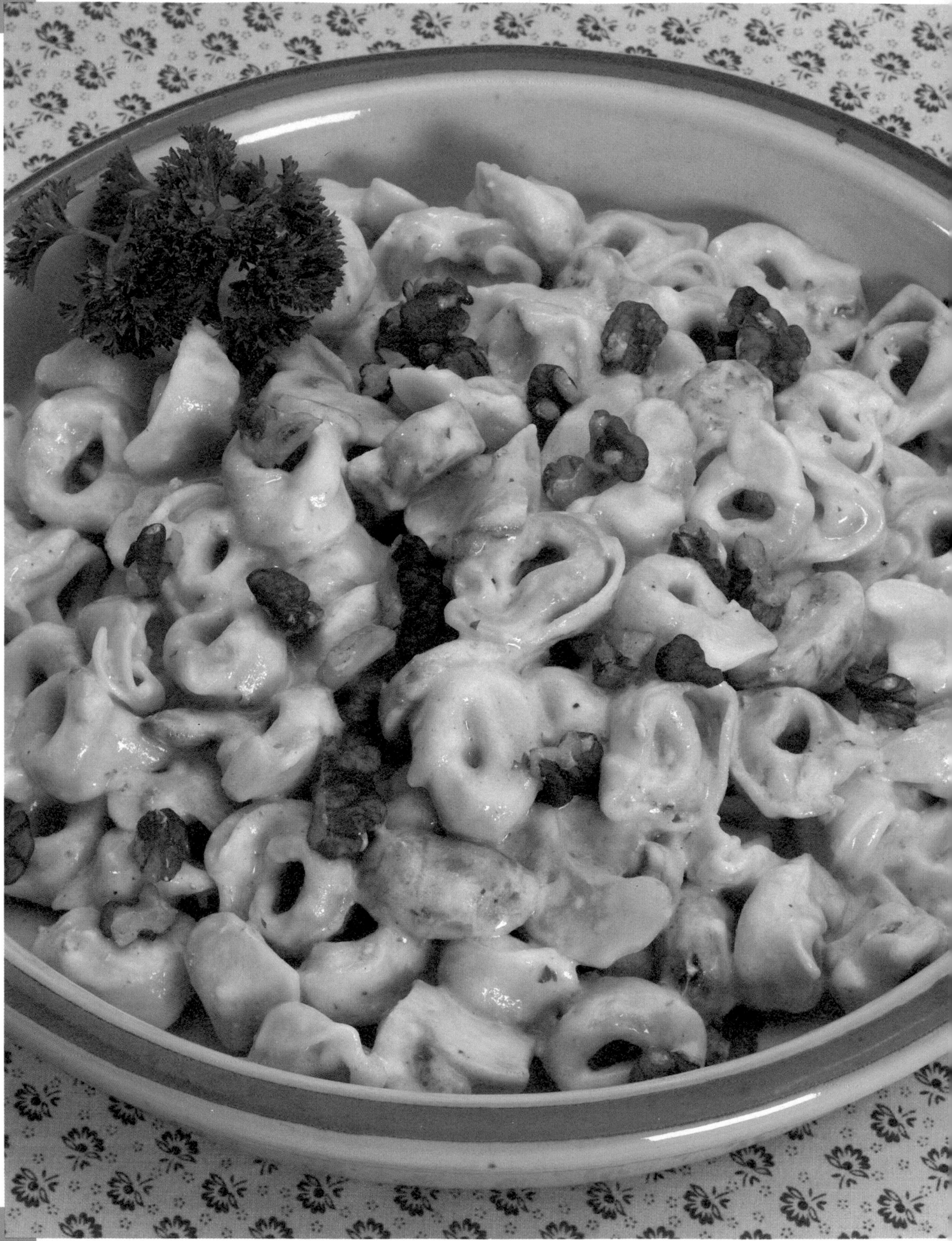

Tortellini with Blue Cheese

(serves 2)

1 SERVING	707 CALORIES	48g CARBOHYDRATE
29g PROTEIN	45g FAT	0.8g FIBER

Setting: HIGH

Cooking time: 7 minutes

Utensil: 12 cups (3 L) casserole

1 tbsp	(15 ml) butter
¼ lb	(125 g) fresh mushrooms, cleaned and sliced thick
½	celery stalk, sliced
1 tsp	(5 ml) chopped fresh parsley
2 oz	(60 g) blue cheese, diced
1 cup	(250 ml) hot white sauce
½ lb	(250 g) package tortellini, cooked and hot
	dash paprika
	salt and pepper
	chopped walnuts for garnish

Place butter, mushrooms, celery and parsley in casserole; cover and microwave 3 minutes.

Stir in blue cheese. Add white sauce and paprika and season well. Microwave 2 minutes, uncovered.

Correct seasoning and stir in pasta; microwave 2 minutes uncovered.

If dcsired sprinkle with chopped walnuts before serving.

Place butter, mushrooms, celery and parsley in casserole; cover and microwave 3 minutes.

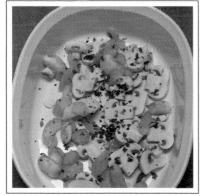

Stir in blue cheese.

Add white sauce and paprika; season well. Microwave 2 minutes uncovered.

Correct seasoning and stir in pasta; microwave 2 minutes uncovered.

Pasta Mélange

(serves 2)

1 SERVING	424 CALORIES	59g CARBOHYDRATE
11g PROTEIN	16g FAT	3.3g FIBER

Setting: HIGH and MEDIUM
Cooking time: 13 minutes
Utensil: 12 cups (3 L) casserole

2 tbsp	(30 ml) olive oil
1	onion, chopped
3	green onions, chopped
½	celery stalk, finely diced
1	tomato, peeled and diced
12	fresh mushrooms, cleaned and halved
1	garlic clove, smashed and chopped
1½ cups	(375 ml) hot tomato sauce
2	portions hot cooked pasta of your choice
	salt and pepper

Place oil, both onions, celery, salt and pepper in casserole. Cover and microwave 4 minutes at HIGH.

Mix well and add tomato, mushrooms and garlic. Season, cover and microwave 3 minutes at HIGH.

Stir in tomato sauce, correct seasoning and microwave 3 minutes uncovered at HIGH.

Add pasta, mix and microwave 3 minutes uncovered at MEDIUM.

Serve with fresh Italian bread if desired.

Quick Macaroni Bite

(serves 2)

1 SERVING	371 CALORIES	72g CARBOHYDRATE
13g PROTEIN	3g FAT	0.8g FIBER

Setting: HIGH and MEDIUM-HIGH
Cooking time: 10 minutes
Utensil: 12 cups (3 L) casserole

3 cups	(750 ml) boiling water
½ tsp	(2 ml) vinegar
1 tsp	(5 ml) olive oil
2 cups	(500 ml) macaroni
¼ cup	(50 ml) grated cheese of your choice
1½ cups	(375 ml) hot tomato sauce
	salt and pepper

Place water, vinegar, oil and salt in casserole. Add pasta and stir well. Microwave 7 minutes uncovered at HIGH, stirring frequently to avoid sticking.

Cover casserole and let pasta stand 8 minutes before draining.

Replace drained and rinsed pasta in casserole. Add remaining ingredients and microwave 3 minutes uncovered at MEDIUM-HIGH.

Macaroni and Eggplant

(serves 2 to 3)

1 SERVING	414 CALORIES	60g CARBOHYDRATE
14g PROTEIN	13g FAT	3.2g FIBER

Setting: HIGH and MEDIUM-HIGH
Cooking time: 18 minutes
Utensil: 12 cups (3 L) casserole

2 tbsp	(30 ml) butter
1	onion, finely chopped
1	garlic clove, smashed and chopped
½	eggplant, diced
2	tomatoes, peeled and diced
½ cup	(125 ml) tomato sauce
4 cups	(1 L) hot, cooked macaroni
½ cup	(125 ml) grated Parmesan cheese
	salt and pepper

Place butter, onion and garlic in casserole. Cover and microwave 3 minutes at HIGH.

Stir in eggplant and tomatoes; season well. Cover and microwave 12 minutes at HIGH.

Stir in tomato sauce and macaroni; correct seasoning. Microwave 3 minutes uncovered at MEDIUM-HIGH.

Serve with grated cheese.

Lamb Chops à la Suzanne

(serves 2)

1 SERVING	402 CALORIES	6g CARBOHYDRATE
50g PROTEIN	20g FAT	2.2g FIBER

Setting: HIGH and MEDIUM-HIGH

Cooking time: 11 minutes (preheating required)

Utensil: browning grill
12 cups (3 L) casserole

4	1¼ in (3 cm) thick lamb chops, lightly oiled
1 tbsp	(15 ml) butter
½	zucchini, sliced
1	celery stalk, diced
1	carrot, pared and diced
1 tbsp	(15 ml) chopped fresh parsley
	salt and pepper

Preheat browning grill
10 minutes in microwave.

Add lamb chops and microwave
3 minutes uncovered at HIGH.

Turn chops over, season and
microwave 3 minutes uncovered
at MEDIUM-HIGH. Remove from
grill and keep warm.

Place all remaining ingredients in
casserole. Cover and microwave
5 minutes at HIGH.

Serve lamb chops with vegetables
and mint jelly.

Parmesan Pork Dinner

(serves 4)

1 SERVING	850 CALORIES	97g CARBOHYDRATE
54g PROTEIN	27g FAT	0.9g FIBER

Setting: HIGH and MEDIUM-HIGH

Cooking time: 13 minutes

Utensil: 12 cups (3 L) casserole

2 tbsp	(30 ml) butter
1	onion, finely chopped
1 lb	(500 g) lean ground pork
5½ oz	(156 ml) can tomato paste
1 tsp	(5 ml) allspice
1 cup	(250 ml) grated Parmesan cheese
1 lb	(500 g) broad egg noodles, cooked
	pinch nutmeg
	salt and pepper

Place butter and onion in casserole. Cover and microwave 2 minutes at HIGH.

Stir in pork and season well; microwave 4 minutes covered at HIGH, stirring several times during cooking process.

Mix in tomato paste, seasonings and cheese; microwave 4 minutes uncovered at MEDIUM-HIGH.

Add noodles, mix well and finish microwaving 3 minutes uncovered at MEDIUM-HIGH.

Smoked Chops with Sauerkraut

(serves 4)

1 SERVING	402 CALORIES	25g CARBOHYDRATE
22g PROTEIN	24g FAT	1.2g FIBER

Setting: HIGH

Cooking time: 43 minutes

Utensil: 12 cups (3 L) casserole

½	onion, chopped
1 tbsp	(15 ml) bacon fat
1 tbsp	(15 ml) chopped fresh parsley
1	clove
4	medium potatoes, peeled
½	28 oz (796 ml) can sauerkraut, rinsed
¼ cup	(50 ml) dry white wine
¼ cup	(50 ml) hot chicken stock
4	smoked pork chops
	salt and pepper

Place onion, bacon fat, parsley and clove in casserole; cover and microwave 3 minutes.

Add remaining ingredients, except pork, and microwave 30 minutes covered.

Add chops, correct seasoning and finish microwaving 10 minutes uncovered.

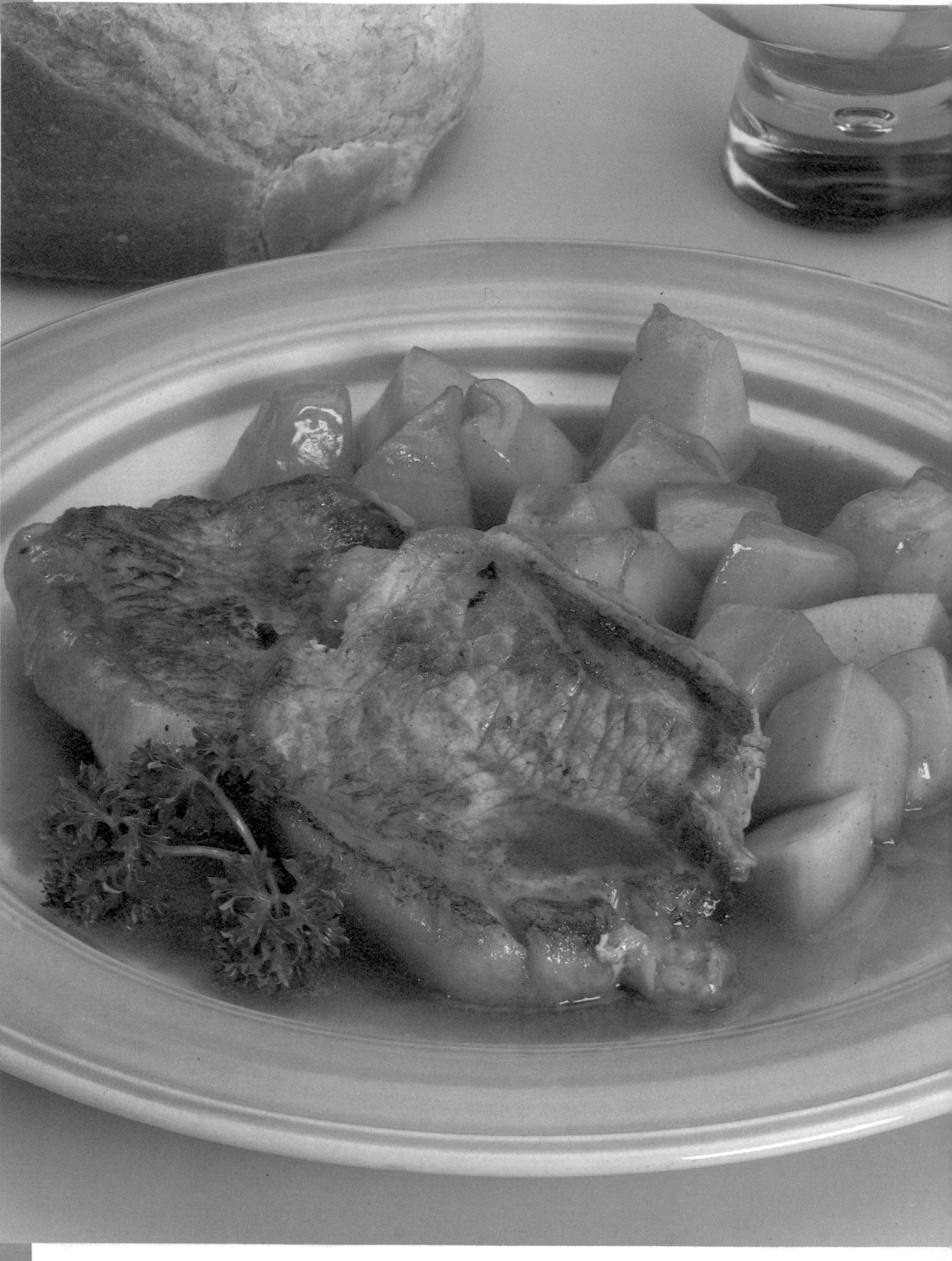

Butterflied Pork Chops Lizanne

(serves 2)

1 SERVING	295 CALORIES	3g CARBOHYDRATE
35g PROTEIN	16g FAT	0g FIBER

Setting: HIGH and MEDIUM-HIGH

Cooking time: 4 minutes (preheating required)

Utensil: browning grill

1 tsp	(5 ml) vegetable oil
1 tsp	(5 ml) soya sauce
1 tsp	(5 ml) honey
2	butterflied pork chops
½ tsp	(2 ml) peanut oil
	salt and pepper

Mix vegetable oil with soya sauce and honey.

Slash fat on chops to prevent curling during cooking. Brush marinade on both sides of meat and set aside.

Preheat browning grill 10 minutes in microwave.

Add chops and microwave 2 minutes uncovered at HIGH.

Brush chops with peanut oil, turn them over, season and finish microwaving 2 minutes uncovered at MEDIUM-HIGH.

Serve with vegetables or sautéed melon in sauce.

Roast Pork Loin

(serves 4)

1 SERVING	614 CALORIES	1g CARBOHYDRATE
81g PROTEIN	32g FAT	0g FIBER

Setting: MEDIUM

Cooking time: 36 minutes (preheating required)

Utensil: browning grill

3 lb	(1.4 kg) loin of pork, boned, fat trimmed and rolled
1	garlic clove, peeled and cut into 3 slivers
1 tbsp	(15 ml) vegetable oil
1 tbsp	(15 ml) soya sauce
1 tsp	(5 ml) honey
	salt and pepper

Using paring knife, cut deep incisions in pork and insert garlic slivers.

Mix oil, soya sauce and honey together; brush all over meat.

Preheat browning grill 10 minutes in microwave.

Add pork, season and cover with waxed paper. Microwave 18 minutes.

Turn roast over, season, cover and continue microwaving 18 minutes.

Remove waxed paper and let stand 12 minutes before serving.

Roast Pork Tenderloin

(serves 2)

1 SERVING	305 CALORIES	2g CARBOHYDRATE
23g PROTEIN	23g FAT	0g FIBER

Setting: MEDIUM

Cooking time: 7 minutes (preheating required)

Utensil: browning grill

1	pork tenderloin, fat removed and split lengthwise
1 tbsp	(15 ml) catsup
1 tbsp	(15 ml) vegetable oil
1 tbsp	(15 ml) soya sauce
1	garlic clove, smashed and chopped
1 tbsp	(15 ml) finely chopped fresh ginger
	salt and pepper

Place pork on large plate and set aside.

Mix catsup, oil and remaining ingredients together in small bowl. Season to taste.

Brush mixture generously over pork on both sides.

Preheat browning grill 10 minutes in microwave.

Add meat, cover with waxed paper and microwave 4 minutes.

Turn tenderloin over, cover and microwave another 3 minutes.

Serve with vegetables and if desired, a spicy sauce.

Pork Stew

(serves 4)

1 SERVING	405 CALORIES	12g CARBOHYDRATE
38g PROTEIN	23g FAT	1.0g FIBER

Setting: MEDIUM-HIGH
Cooking time: 1 hour 8 minutes
Utensil: 12 cups (3 L) casserole

1½ lb	(750 g) cubed pork shoulder
1 tsp	(5 ml) oil
1 tbsp	(15 ml) soya sauce
1 tsp	(5 ml) Worcestershire sauce
1 tsp	(5 ml) maple syrup
1	onion, chopped
1	garlic clove, smashed and chopped
1 tsp	(5 ml) chopped fresh parsley
¼ tsp	(1 ml) rosemary
½ tsp	(2 ml) oregano
28 oz	(796 ml) can tomatoes, drained and chopped
1 cup	(250 ml) hot beef stock
¼ cup	(50 ml) Folonari Valpolicella red wine
	salt and pepper

Place pork in casserole with oil, soya sauce, Worcestershire sauce and maple syrup.

Add onion, garlic and seasonings. Cover and microwave 8 minutes.

Mix well and add remaining ingredients; season well. Cover and microwave 1 hour, mixing occasionally.

Serve with a side dish of egg noodles.

Have ready 1½ lb (750 g) cubed pork shoulder.

Place in casserole with oil, soya sauce, Worcestershire sauce and maple syrup.

Add onion, garlic and seasonings. Cover and microwave 8 minutes.

Mix well and add remaining ingredients; season well. Cover and microwave 1 hour, mixing occasionally.

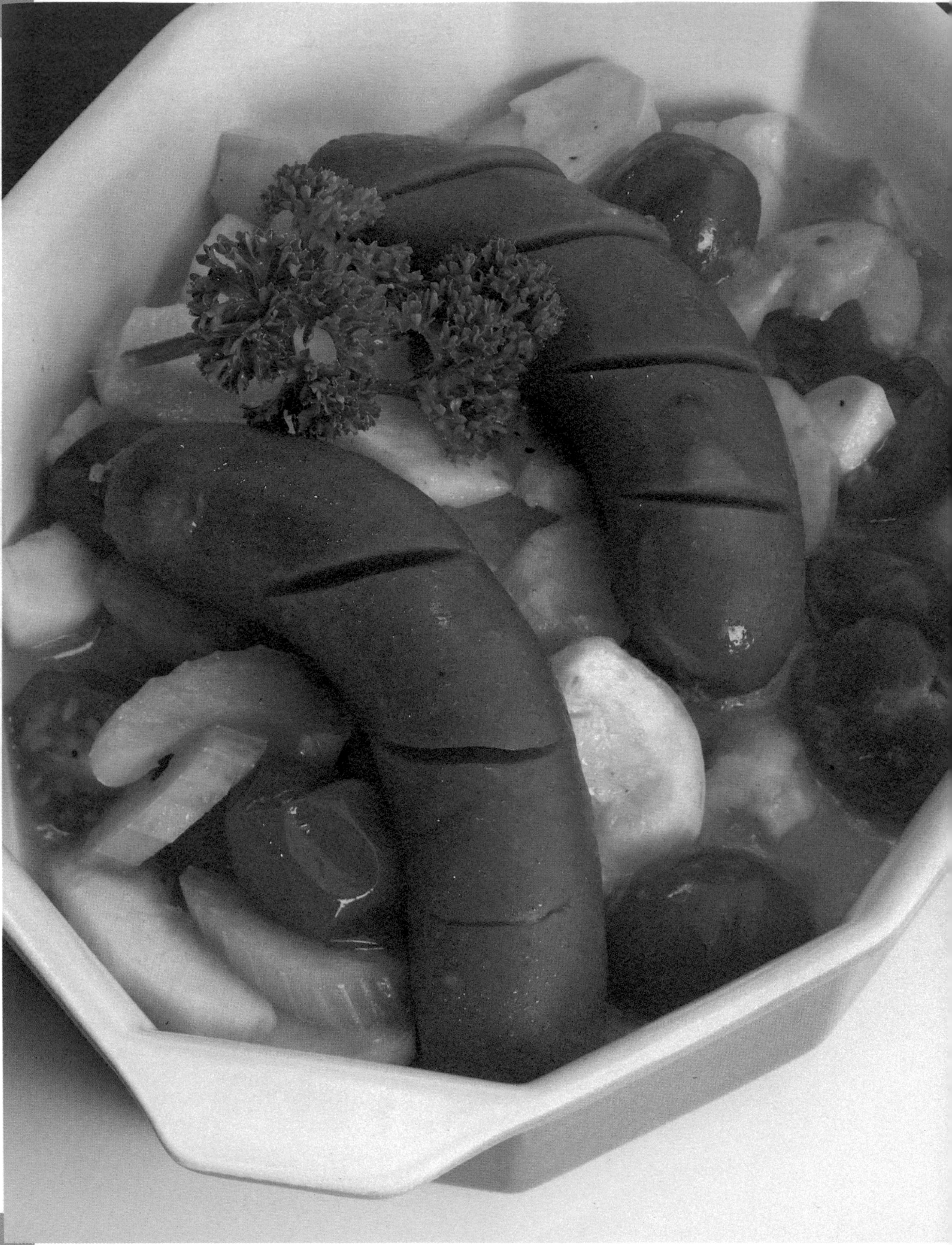

Sausages on Veggy Bed

(serves 2)

1 SERVING	464 CALORIES	43g CARBOHYDRATE
15g PROTEIN	26g FAT	4.1g FIBER

Setting: HIGH and MEDIUM-HIGH

Cooking time: 10 minutes

Utensil: 12 cups (3 L) casserole

1	celery stalk, sliced thick
2	apples, cored, peeled and sliced thick
1 cup	(250 ml) sliced yellow squash
1 tsp	(5 ml) paprika
1 tbsp	(15 ml) butter
2 tbsp	(30 ml) flour
6	cherry tomatoes, halved
¾ cup	(175 ml) hot chicken stock
2	knackwurst sausages, scored
	salt and pepper

Place celery, apples, squash, paprika and butter in casserole.

Mix in flour and season well.

Add tomatoes and pour in chicken stock; microwave 5 minutes uncovered at HIGH.

Stir well, correct seasoning and set sausages on vegetables. Cover and microwave 5 minutes at MEDIUM-HIGH.

Place celery, apples, squash, paprika and butter in casserole.

Mix in flour and season well.

Add tomatoes and pour in chicken stock; microwave 5 minutes uncovered at HIGH.

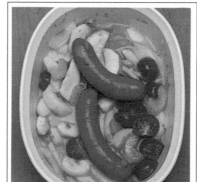
Stir well, correct seasoning and set sausages on vegetables. Cover and microwave 5 minutes at MEDIUM-HIGH.

Ham Steaks with Onion Purée

(serves 4)

1 SERVING	281 CALORIES	16g CARBOHYDRATE
25g PROTEIN	13g FAT	0.5g FIBER

Setting: HIGH

Cooking time: 13½ minutes

Utensil: 12 cups (3 L) casserole browning grill

3	onions, halved and sliced
1 tbsp	(15 ml) butter
1 tsp	(5 ml) chopped fresh parsley

½ cup	(125 ml) water
2 tbsp	(30 ml) flour
1 tbsp	(15 ml) paprika
1¼ cups	(300 ml) hot chicken stock
1 tsp	(5 ml) oil
2 tbsp	(30 ml) maple syrup
1 tsp	(5 ml) soya sauce
4	¼ in (0.65 cm) thick ham steaks
	salt and pepper

Place onions, butter, parsley, water, flour and paprika in casserole; mix and microwave 10 minutes, covered.

Pour in chicken stock, correct seasoning and mix well; microwave 3 minutes uncovered.

Pour onion mixture into food processor and purée.

Mix oil with maple syrup and soya sauce; brush over both sides of ham steaks.

Preheat browning grill 10 minutes in microwave.

Add ham and microwave 30 seconds uncovered.

Turn pieces over and let stand another 30 seconds.

Serve with onion purée.

Place onions, butter, parsley and water in casserole.

Pour in chicken stock, correct seasoning and mix well; microwave 3 minutes uncovered.

Add flour and paprika, mix and microwave 10 minutes, covered.

Pour onion mixture into food processor and purée.

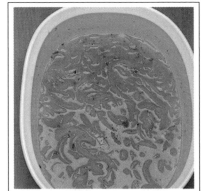

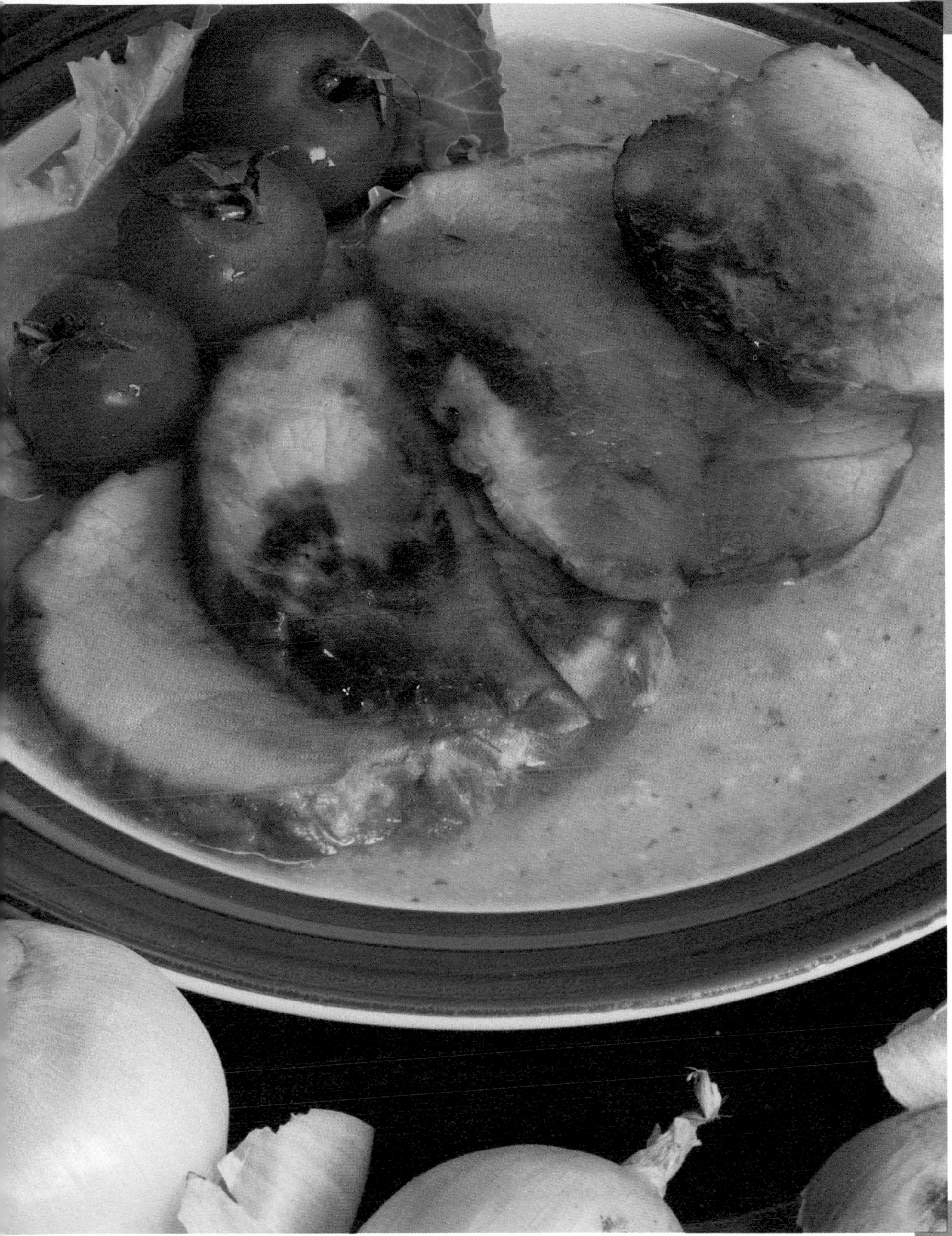

Rolled Ham Parmesan

(serves 4)

1 SERVING	212 CALORIES	8g CARBOHYDRATE
16g PROTEIN	13g FAT	0.5g FIBER

Setting: HIGH and MEDIUM-HIGH

Cooking time: 15 minutes

Utensil: 12 cups (3 L) casserole
6 cups (1.5 L) square dish

2 tbsp	(30 ml) butter
1 tbsp	(15 ml) chopped shallots
½ lb	(250 g) fresh mushrooms, cleaned and finely chopped
2 tbsp	(30 ml) Folonari Chardonnay white wine
1 cup	(250 ml) hot beef stock
1 tsp	(5 ml) soya sauce
1½ tbsp	(25 ml) cornstarch
3 tbsp	(45 ml) cold water
8	large, thin slices Black Forest ham
½ cup	(125 ml) grated Parmesan cheese
	salt and pepper

Place butter, shallots, mushrooms, salt and pepper in casserole. Microwave 4 minutes uncovered at HIGH.

Pour in wine, beef stock and soya sauce; continue microwaving 4 minutes.

Mix cornstarch with water; stir into sauce and mix very well. Microwave 4 minutes uncovered at HIGH, stirring halfway through. Set aside to cool slightly.

Spread thin layer of mushroom mixture over ham slices. Carefully roll and place in buttered square dish.

Pour in leftover sauce, top with cheese and season; microwave 3 minutes uncovered at MEDIUM-HIGH.

Pork-Stuffed Grapevine Leaves

(serves 4)

1 SERVING	483 CALORIES	27g CARBOHYDRATE
38g PROTEIN	25g FAT	0.9g FIBER

Setting: HIGH and MEDIUM-HIGH

Cooking time: 14 minutes

Utensil: 12 cups (3 L) casserole
6 cups (1.5 L) square dish

2 tbsp	(30 ml) butter
1	onion, finely chopped
1	garlic clove, smashed and chopped
1¼ lb	(625 g) lean ground pork
5½ oz	(156 ml) can tomato paste
1 cup	(250 ml) cooked rice
2 cups	(500 ml) hot thin tomato sauce
4 tbsp	(60 ml) grated Parmesan cheese
	pinch mint
	jar grapevine leaves, drained and rinsed
	salt and pepper

Place 1 tbsp (15 ml) butter in casserole. Add onion and garlic; cover and microwave 3 minutes at HIGH.

Add pork and mix well; season. Cover and microwave 4 minutes at HIGH, mixing once during cooking.

Add tomato paste and rice; mix well and correct seasoning. Add mint. Microwave 2 minutes covered at HIGH.

Season and spread mixture over doubled grapevine leaves. Roll and place bundles in buttered square dish. Pour in tomato sauce, top with cheese and microwave 5 minutes uncovered at MEDIUM-HIGH.

Veal Chops with Tomato Fondue

(serves 2)

1 SERVING	333 CALORIES	14g CARBOHYDRATE
27g PROTEIN	19g FAT	1.2g FIBER

Setting: HIGH

Cooking time: 21 minutes (preheating required)

Utensil: 12 cups (3 L) casserole browning grill

1 tbsp	(15 ml) olive oil	
½	celery stalk, diced	
½	small onion, diced	
1	garlic clove, smashed and chopped	
1 tbsp	(15 ml) chopped fresh parsley	
½	28 oz (796 ml) can tomatoes, drained and chopped	
2 tbsp	(30 ml) tomato paste	
2	veal chops, lightly oiled	
	pinch sugar	
	salt and pepper	
	few drops hot pepper sauce	

Place oil, celery, onion, garlic and parsley in casserole. Cover and microwave 4 minutes.

Mix in tomatoes, sugar and season well. Stir in tomato paste, hot pepper sauce and microwave 15 minutes uncovered. Set aside.

Preheat browning grill 10 minutes in microwave.

Add veal and microwave 30 seconds, uncovered.

Season and turn chops over; continue microwaving 1 minute. Season again, turn chops over and finish microwaving 30 seconds.

Sweetbread Vol-au-Vent

(serves 6 to 8)

1 SERVING	393 CALORIES	18g CARBOHYDRATE
14g PROTEIN	30g FAT	0.2g FIBER

Setting: HIGH
Cooking time: 13 minutes
Utensil: 12 cups (3 L) casserole

1 tbsp	(15 ml) butter
½ lb	(250 g) sweetbreads cooked and diced
12	fresh mushrooms, cleaned and diced small
1 tbsp	(15 ml) chopped fresh parsley
1 tsp	(5 ml) tarragon
2 oz	(60 g) feta cheese, cut up
1 cup	(250 ml) hot thick white sauce
18	mini vol-au-vent shells, cooked and still hot
	salt and pepper
	dash paprika

Place butter, sweetbreads, mushrooms, parsley and tarragon in casserole; cover and microwave 4 minutes.

Season well and add paprika. Add feta cheese.

Pour in white sauce and mix well; microwave 8 minutes uncovered.

Fill vol-au-vent shells with mixture and microwave 1 minute uncovered.

Place butter, sweetbreads, mushrooms, parsley and tarragon in casserole; cover and microwave 4 minutes.

Pour in white sauce and mix well. Microwave 8 minutes uncovered.

Season well and add paprika. Add feta cheese.

Fill vol-au-vent shells and microwave 1 minute uncovered.

Budget Veal

(serves 4)

1 SERVING	421 CALORIES	14g CARBOHYDRATE
40g PROTEIN	23g FAT	2.5g FIBER

Setting: HIGH
Cooking time: 8 minutes
Utensil: 12 cups (3 L) casserole

3 tbsp	(45 ml) butter
2 lb	(900 g) veal cutlets, cut into strips
3 tbsp	(45 ml) seasoned flour
1	celery stalk, sliced
1½ cups	(375 ml) hot beef stock
1½ cups	(375 ml) bean sprouts
12	cherry tomatoes, halved
1 tbsp	(15 ml) soya sauce
12	snow pea pods, pared
1	garlic clove, smashed and chopped
	salt and pepper

Place butter in casserole and microwave 1 minute uncovered.

Dredge meat in flour and add to casserole. Microwave 2 minutes uncovered, stirring once or twice.

Add celery, beef stock and season well. Microwave 2 minutes uncovered.

Add remaining ingredients, mix well and correct seasoning. Microwave 3 minutes uncovered.

Beef and Vegetable Stew

(serves 4)

1 SERVING	321 CALORIES	9g CARBOHYDRATE
44g PROTEIN	12g FAT	1.1g FIBER

Setting: MEDIUM
Cooking time: 1 hour
Utensil: 12 cups (3 L) casserole

1½ lb	(750 g) cubed stewing beef
1	carrot, pared and sliced
1 cup	(250 ml) dry red wine
2 tbsp	(30 ml) chopped fresh parsley
½	onion, sliced
1½ cups	(375 ml) hot brown sauce
2	garlic cloves, smashed and chopped
¼ tsp	(1 ml) celery seeds
¼ tsp	(1 ml) thyme
½ tsp	(2 ml) tarragon
½ lb	(250 g) fresh mushrooms, cleaned
	salt and pepper

Place beef, carrot, wine, half of parsley and onion in bowl; marinate 15 minutes.

Transfer contents to casserole and stir in brown sauce, garlic and seasonings. Cover and microwave 50 minutes.

Add mushrooms and correct seasoning; cover and finish microwaving 10 minutes.

Serve sprinkled with chopped fresh parsley if desired.

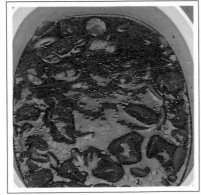 **1** lace beef, carrot, wine, half of parsley and onion in bowl; marinate 15 minutes.

3 Add garlic and seasonings. Cover and microwave 50 minutes.

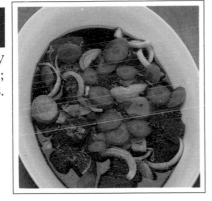 **2** ransfer contents to casserole and stir in brown sauce.

 **4** Add mushrooms and correct seasoning; cover and finish microwaving 10 minutes.

Beef Goulash

(serves 4)

1 SERVING	440 CALORIES	22g CARBOHYDRATE
43g PROTEIN	20g FAT	1.6g FIBER

Setting: HIGH and MEDIUM
Cooking time: 1 hour (preheating required)
Utensil: browning grill
12 cups (3 L) casserole

2 tbsp	(30 ml) vegetable oil
1½ lb	(750 g) cubed stewing beef (blade steak)
2 tbsp	(30 ml) paprika
½	onion, chopped
1	sweet potato, peeled and cubed
2	carrots, pared and cubed
1	onion, peeled and quartered
1 tbsp	(15 ml) chopped fresh parsley
2 cups	(500 ml) hot brown sauce
2 tbsp	(30 ml) tomato paste
1	garlic clove, smashed and chopped
¼ tsp	(1 ml) thyme
1	bay leaf
	salt and pepper

Preheat browning grill 10 minutes in microwave.

Brush meat with 1 tbsp (15 ml) oil. Add half of meat to browning grill. Let stand 1 minute, turning cubes to sear all sides. Remove and set aside.

Repeat process (including preheating) for rest of meat.

When all meat has been seared, sprinkle with 1 tbsp (15 ml) paprika.

Place remaining oil in casserole. Add chopped onion, remaining paprika and beef.

Add all vegetables and parsley. Pour in brown sauce, mix in tomato paste, garlic, thyme and bay leaf; season well.

Cover and microwave 50 minutes at MEDIUM.

Uncover and finish microwaving 10 minutes.

Brush meat with **1** 1 tbsp (15 ml) oil.

When all meat **2** has been seared, sprinkle with 1 tbsp (15 ml) paprika.

3 Place remaining oil in casserole. Add chopped onion, remaining paprika and beef.

4 Add all vegetables and parsley.

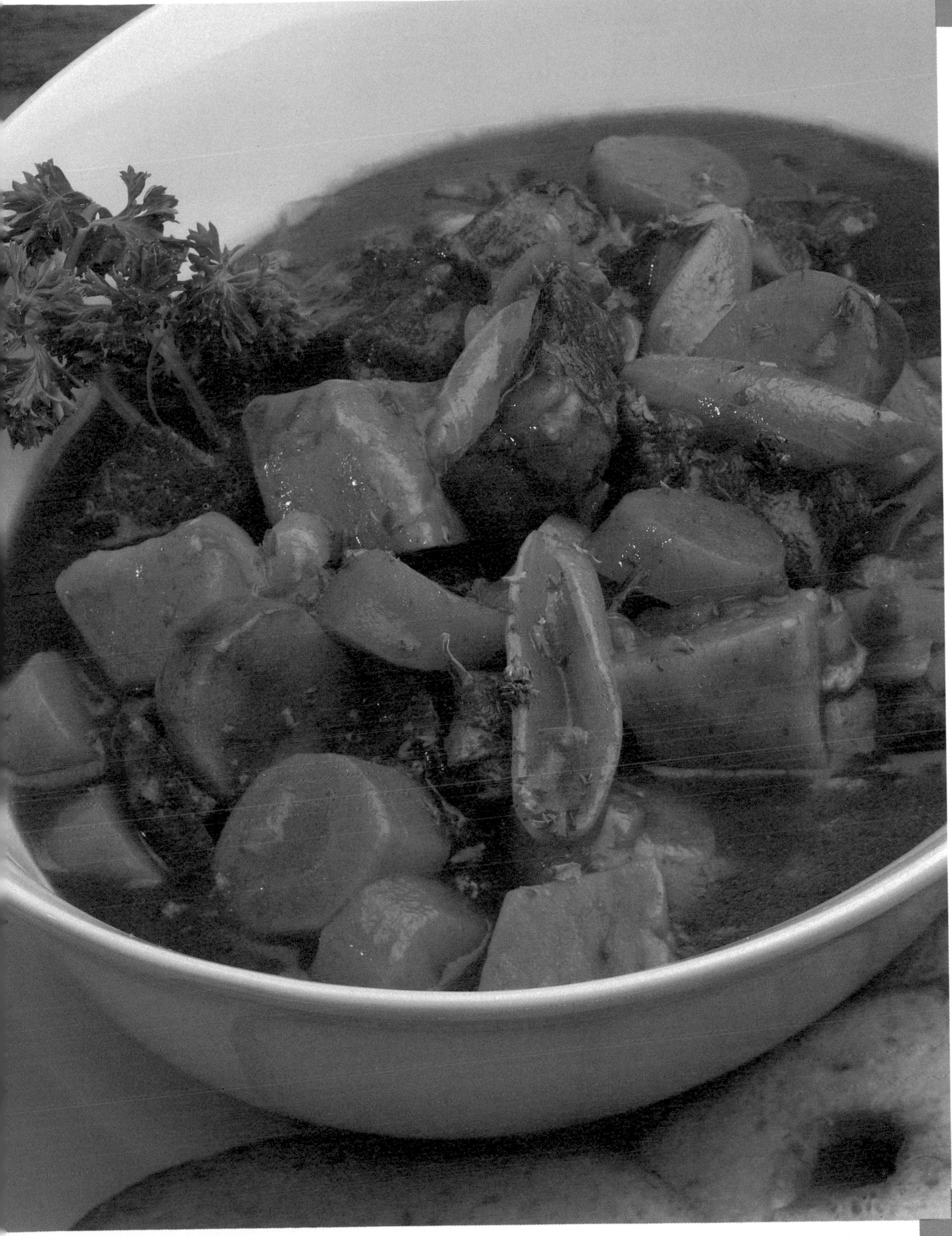

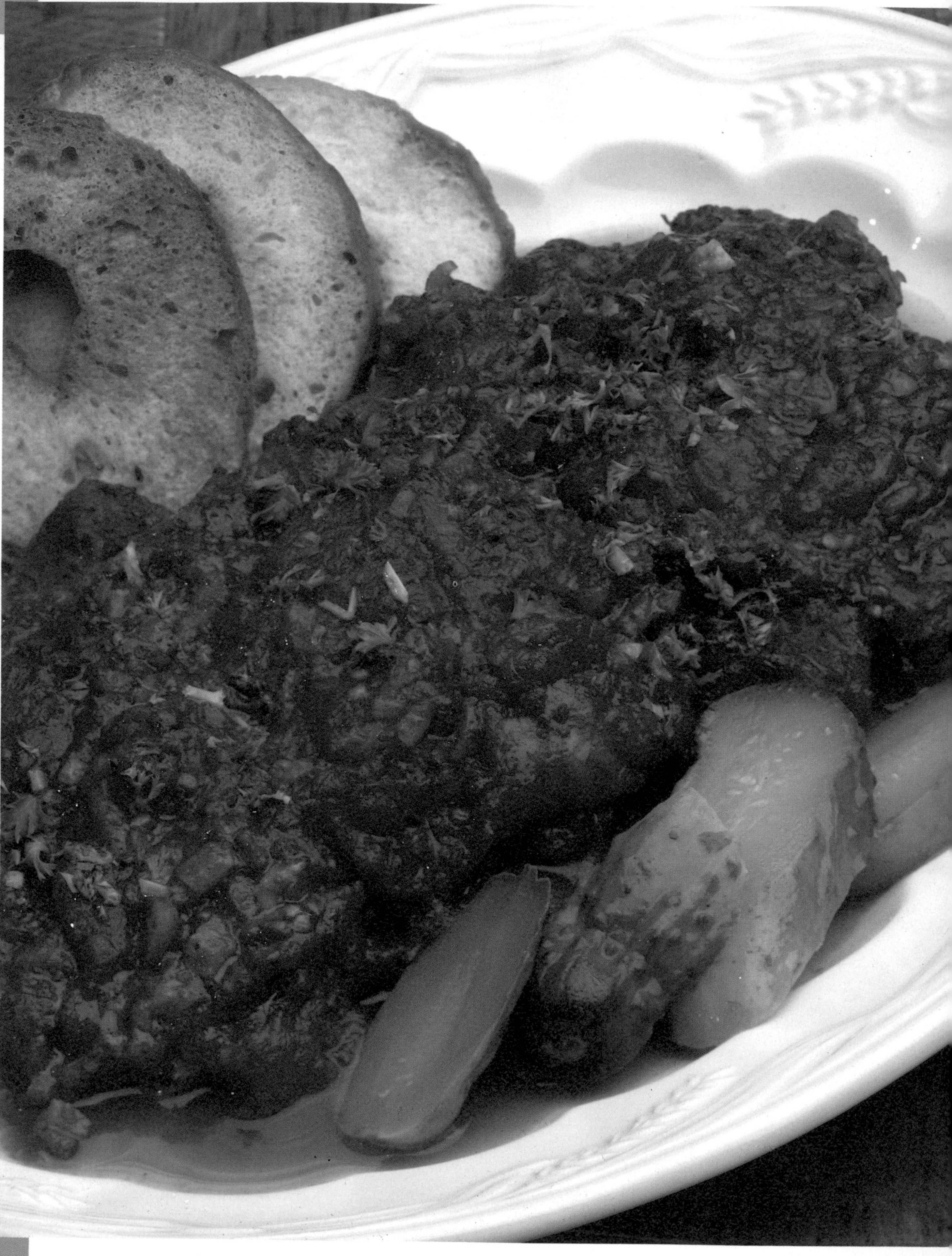

Braised Flank Steak

(serves 4)

1 SERVING	626 CALORIES	17g CARBOHYDRATE
68g PROTEIN	32g FAT	1.1g FIBER

Setting: HIGH and MEDIUM
Cooking time: 1 hour 2 minutes
Utensil: 8 cups (2 L) rectangular dish

2½ lb	(1.2 kg) flank steak
2 tbsp	(30 ml) vegetable oil
1	large onion, chopped
1 tbsp	(15 ml) soya sauce
1 tbsp	(15 ml) maple syrup
28 oz	(796 ml) can tomatoes (with juice)
1 tbsp	(15 ml) chopped fresh parsley
2	garlic cloves, smashed and chopped
½ tsp	(2 ml) oregano
½ tsp	(2 ml) marjoram
3 tbsp	(45 ml) tomato paste
	salt and pepper
	pinch sugar

Trim fat from flank steak and slice, on an angle, into pieces ¼-½ in (0.65-1.2 cm) thick.

Place 1 tbsp (15 ml) oil and onion in rectangular dish; cover with plastic wrap and microwave 2 minutes at HIGH.

Place meat on onion. Mix soya sauce with remaining oil and maple syrup; brush over meat and season.

Add tomatoes and remaining ingredients; season well. Cover with plastic wrap and microwave 50 minutes at MEDIUM.

Uncover and finish microwaving 10 minutes.

Trim fat from flank steak and slice, on an angle, into pieces ½-¼ in (0.65-1.2 cm) thick.

Rest meat on cooked onion in rectangular dish. Mix soya sauce with remaining oil and maple syrup; brush over meat and season.

Add tomatoes.

Add remaining ingredients and microwave.

Baby Beef Liver and Bacon

(serves 4)

1 SERVING	221 CALORIES	9g CARBOHYDRATE
22g PROTEIN	11g FAT	0.7g FIBER

Setting: HIGH
Cooking time: 16½ minutes
Utensil: trivet
12 cups (3 L) casserole
8 cups (2 L) rectangular dish

4	slices bacon
1	large onion, thinly sliced
1	garlic clove, smashed and chopped
1	small zucchini, thinly sliced
1 tbsp	(15 ml) chopped fresh parsley
4	slices baby beef liver
	salt and pepper

Place bacon on trivet and microwave 3 minutes uncovered. Pat slices dry and crumble; set aside.

Pour bacon fat into casserole. Add onion and cover; microwave 7 minutes.

Stir in garlic, zucchini and parsley; season well. Microwave 3 minutes covered.

Season liver well and arrange in rectangular dish. Spoon onion mixture over liver and season; microwave 2 minutes 30 seconds uncovered.

Turn slices over, add bacon and microwave 1 minute uncovered.

Strips of Beef with Rice

(serves 4)

1 SERVING	493 CALORIES	49g CARBOHYDRATE
40g PROTEIN	15g FAT	0.9g FIBER

Setting: HIGH
Cooking time: 20½ minutes
Utensil: 12 cups (3 L) casserole

3 tbsp	(45 ml) butter
1¼ lb	(625 g) round steak, cut in strips
1 tbsp	(15 ml) soya sauce
1 tsp	(5 ml) honey
1 cup	(250 ml) long grain rice, rinsed
28 oz	(796 ml) can tomatoes
1 cup	(250 ml) hot chicken stock
	salt and pepper
	paprika to taste

Place butter in casserole and microwave 1 minute uncovered.

Add meat, soya sauce, honey and pepper; mix well. Microwave 4 minutes uncovered, stirring halfway through.

Remove meat and set aside on plate.

Add rice, tomatoes and chicken stock to casserole. Season with paprika, pepper and some salt. Cover and microwave 15 minutes or until rice is cooked.

Fluff rice with fork and stir in beef. Microwave 30 seconds uncovered to reheat.

Beans & Pods Garden Style

(serves 4)

1 SERVING	40 CALORIES	8g CARBOHYDRATE
2g PROTEIN	0g FAT	2.4g FIBER

Setting: HIGH
Cooking time: 12½ minutes
Utensil: 12 cups (3 L) casserole

¼ lb	(125 g) green beans, pared
¼ lb	(125 g) yellow beans, pared
1 cup	(250 ml) hot water
¼ lb	(125 g) snow pea pods
	salt and pepper

Place beans and water in casserole; season well. Cover and microwave 8½ minutes.

Stir in pea pods; cover and microwave 4 minutes.

Drain vegetables and serve.

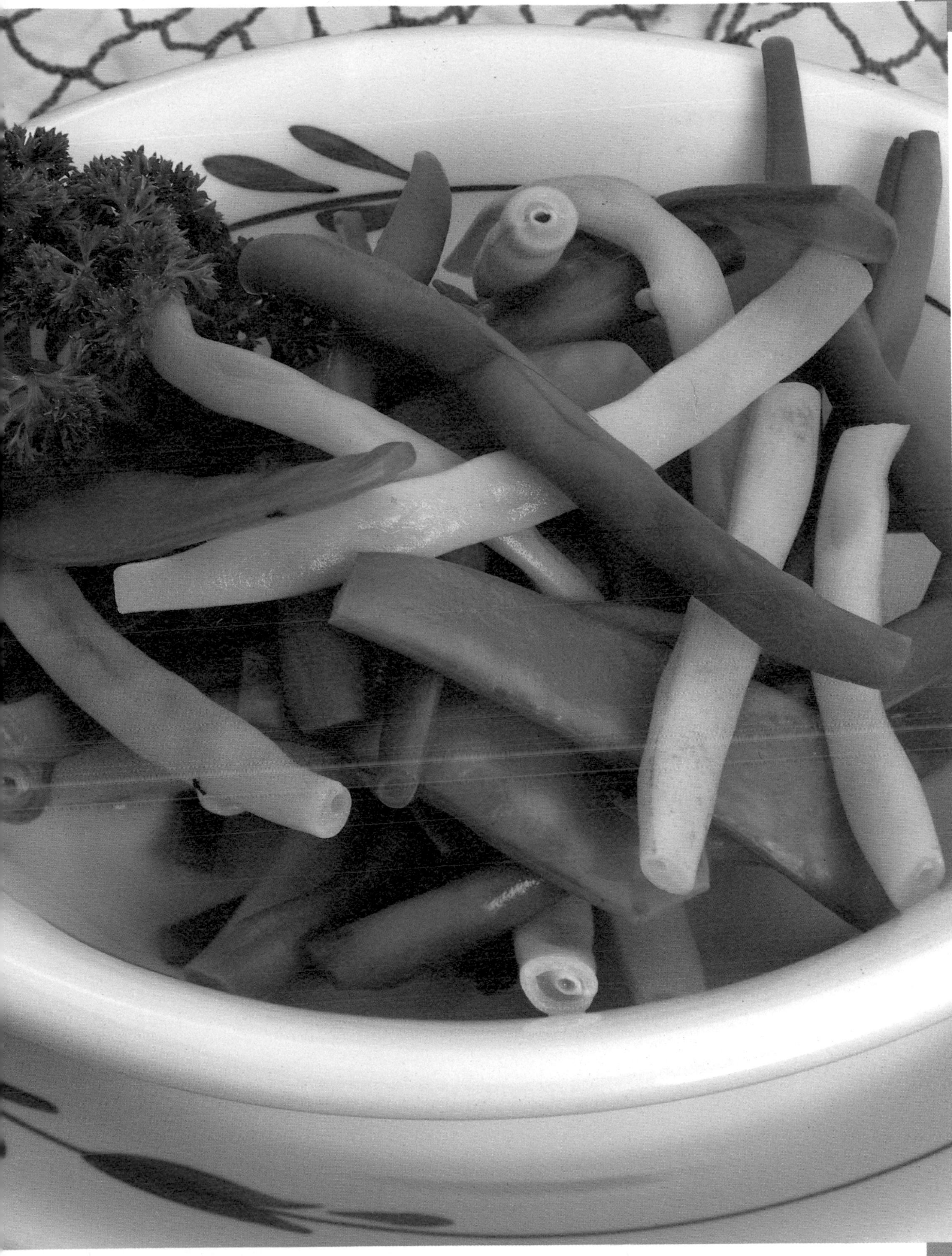

Glazed Sweet Potatoes

(serves 4)

1 SERVING	233 CALORIES	47g CARBOHYDRATE
4g PROTEIN	3g FAT	2.1g FIBER

Setting: HIGH

Cooking time: 5 minutes

Utensil: 8 cups (2 L) rectangular dish

3	large sweet potatoes, peeled and cut in ½ in (1.2 cm) slices
1 tbsp	(15 ml) maple syrup
¼ cup	(50 ml) brown sugar
1 tbsp	(15 ml) grated orange rind
¼ cup	(50 ml) pineapple juice
1 tbsp	(15 ml) butter
1 tsp	(5 ml) cornstarch
2 tbsp	(30 ml) cold water
	juice 1½ oranges
	salt and pepper

Place sweet potatoes in rectangular dish. Top with maple syrup, brown sugar, orange rind, pineapple juice, orange juice and butter; season well. Microwave 3 minutes uncovered.

Remove sweet potato slices from dish and transfer to serving platter; set aside.

Mix cornstarch with water; stir into sauce. Be sure it is well incorporated. Microwave 2 minutes uncovered.

Pour sauce over sweet potatoes and serve.

Potato Apple Mash

(serves 4)

1 SERVING	248 CALORIES	42g CARBOHYDRATE
4g PROTEIN	7g FAT	2.8g FIBER

Setting: HIGH

Cooking time: 35 minutes

Utensil: 12 cups (3 L) casserole

6	potatoes, peeled and halved
3	apples, cored, peeled and quartered
2 tbsp	(30 ml) butter
¼ cup	(50 ml) hot milk
	salt and pepper

Place potatoes in casserole and pour in enough hot water to cover. Season with salt, cover and microwave 30 minutes.

Drain potatoes and replace in casserole. Add apples, butter and season well. Cover and microwave 5 minutes.

Force mixture through potato ricer or food mill into bowl.

Pour in hot milk and mix very well. Correct seasoning and serve.

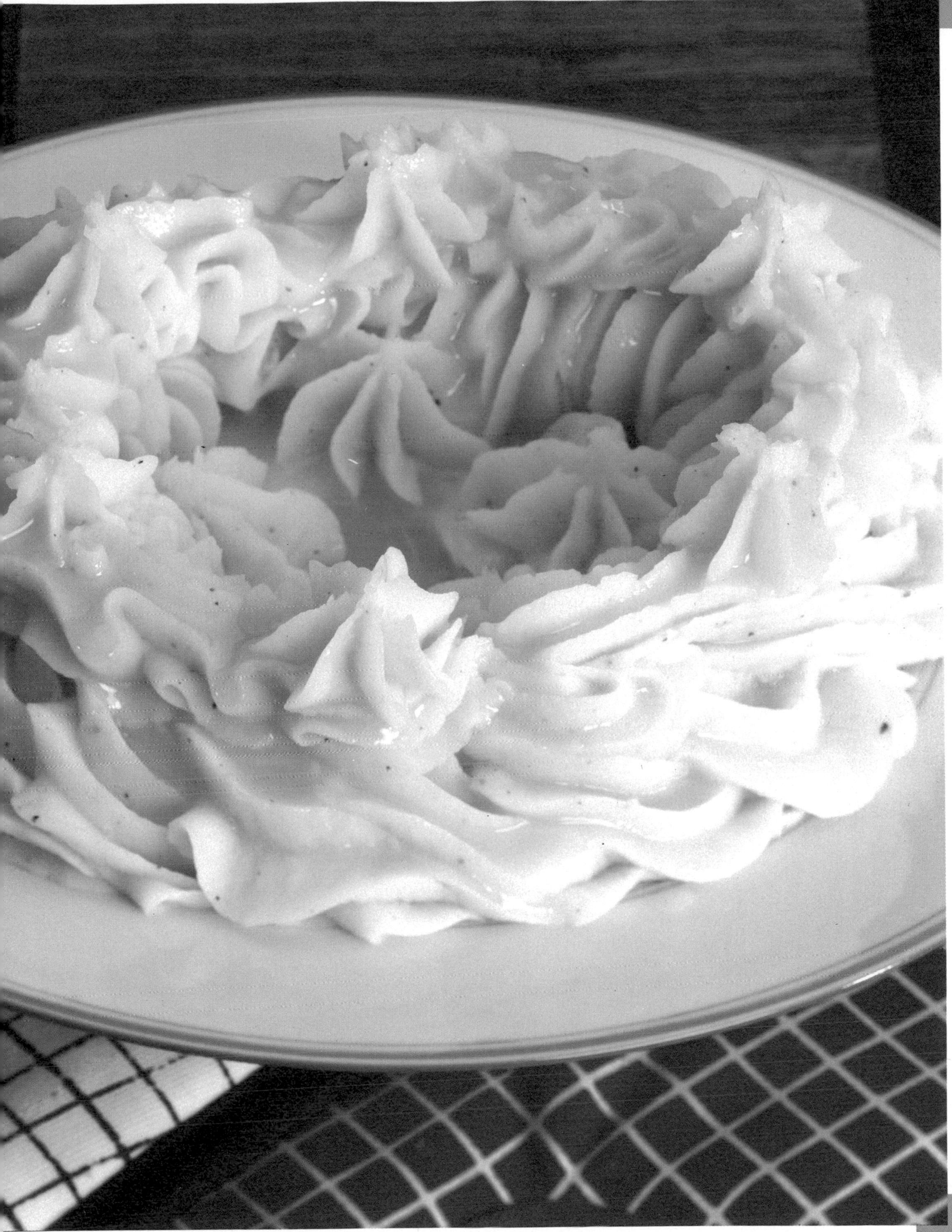

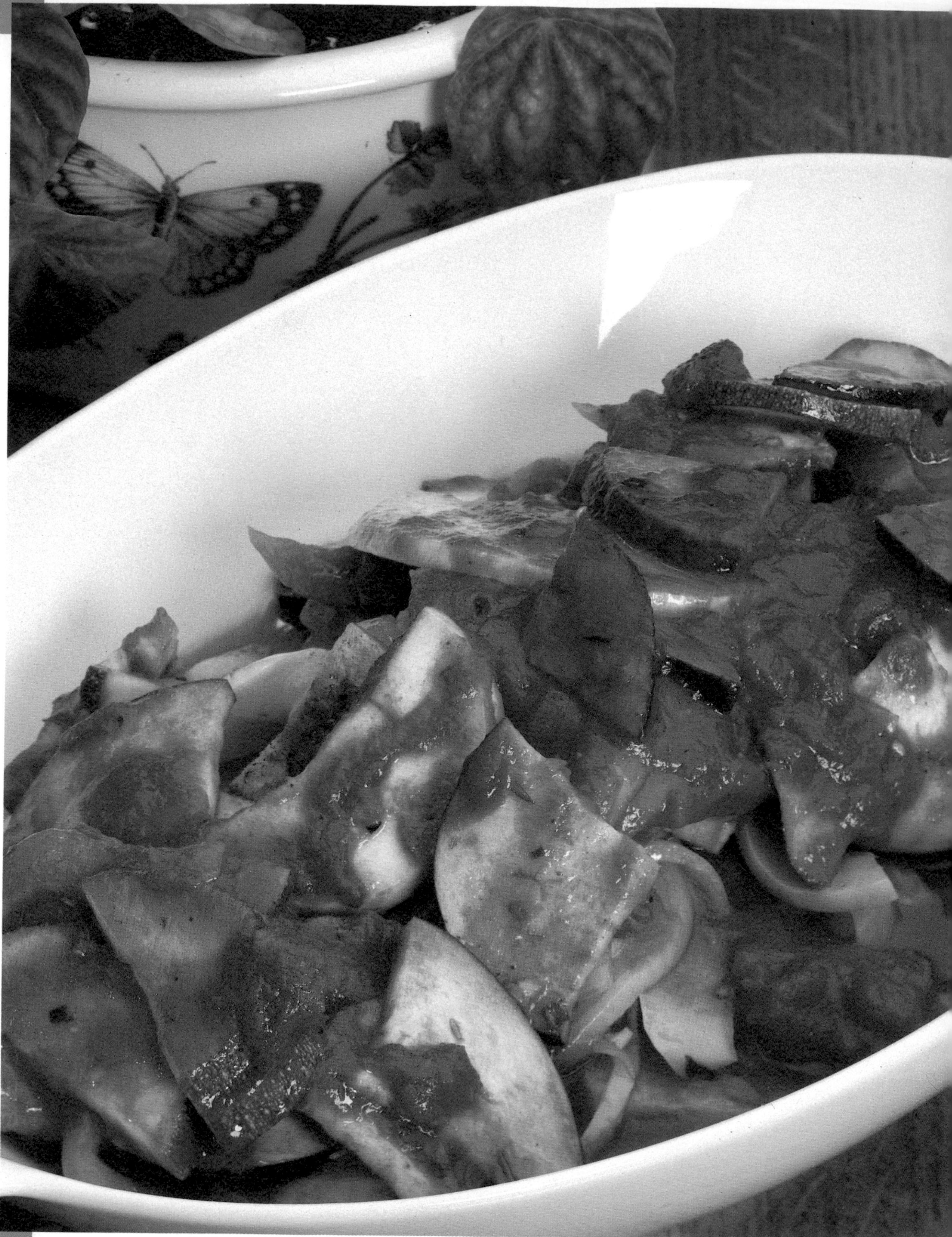

Tomato Vegetable Toss

(serves 4)

1 SERVING	128 CALORIES	20g CARBOHYDRATE
3g PROTEIN	4g FAT	2.5g FIBER

Setting: HIGH

Cooking time: 11 minutes

Utensil: 12 cups (3 L) casserole

1 tbsp	(15 ml) peanut oil
½	yellow pepper, thinly sliced
¼	yellow squash, thinly sliced
½	zucchini, halved lengthwise and sliced
½	eggplant, halved lengthwise and sliced
½	green pepper, thinly sliced
½	onion, thinly sliced
2	garlic cloves, smashed and chopped
¼ tsp	(1 ml) tarragon
¼ tsp	(1 ml) oregano
¼ tsp	(1 ml) thyme
1	leaf fresh sage
1½ cups	(375 ml) hot tomato sauce
	dash paprika
	salt and pepper

Place oil in casserole. Add vegetables, garlic and all seasonings; cover and microwave 5 minutes.

Pour in tomato sauce and mix well. Cover and microwave 6 minutes.

Serve.

Swiss Tomatoes

(serves 4)

1 SERVING	179 CALORIES	8g CARBOHYDRATE
10g PROTEIN	12g FAT	2.7g FIBER

Setting: MEDIUM-HIGH

Cooking time: 7 minutes

Utensil: 6 cups (1.5 L) square dish

1 tbsp	(15 ml) butter
4	large tomatoes, halved crosswise
½ cup	(125 ml) grated Gruyère cheese
½ cup	(125 ml) grated Emmenthal cheese
	salt and pepper
	dash paprika

Grease dish with butter and add tomatoes. Season well and sprinkle on cheese and paprika.

Microwave 4 minutes uncovered.

Rotate dish ¼ turn; continue microwaving 3 minutes.

Carrots with Goat Cheese

(serves 4)

1 SERVING	217 CALORIES	14g CARBOHYDRATE
7g PROTEIN	15g FAT	1.9g FIBER

Setting: HIGH

Cooking time: 12 minutes

Utensil: 12 cups (3 L) casserole

½ lb	(250 g) baby carrots, pared
1	medium onion, diced large
1 tbsp	(15 ml) butter
1 tsp	(5 ml) chopped fresh parsley
¼ cup	(50 ml) goat cheese
1 cup	(250 ml) hot white sauce
	juice ½ lemon
	dash paprika
	dash nutmeg
	salt and pepper

Place carrots and onion in casserole; season well. Add butter, parsley and lemon juice; cover and microwave 7 minutes.

Add cheese in little clumps and season with paprika. Pour in white sauce and add nutmeg; cover and microwave 5 minutes.

Place carrots and onion in casserole; season well.

Add cheese in little clumps and season with paprika.

Add butter, parsley and lemon juice; cover and microwave 7 minutes.

Pour in white sauce, add nutmeg and microwave 5 minutes covered.

French Peas with Lettuce

(serves 4)

1 SERVING	167 CALORIES	20g CARBOHYDRATE
4g PROTEIN	8g FAT	4.7g FIBER

Setting: HIGH and MEDIUM-HIGH

Cooking time: 13 minutes

Utensil: 12 cups (3 L) casserole

3 tbsp	(45 ml) butter
½ tsp	(2 ml) chervil
18	pearl onions
2 tbsp	(30 ml) flour
1	small Boston lettuce, washed, dried and shredded
1 tsp	(5 ml) sugar
14 oz	(398 ml) can French baby peas
	salt and white pepper

Place butter, chervil and onions in casserole. Cover and microwave 7 minutes at HIGH.

Mix in flour until well incorporated. Add lettuce, sugar and season well; microwave 3 minutes covered at HIGH.

Stir in peas with juice. Microwave 3 minutes uncovered at MEDIUM-HIGH.

Eggplant à la Grecque

(serves 4)

1 SERVING	267 CALORIES	19g CARBOHYDRATE
1g PROTEIN	21g FAT	2.9g FIBER

Setting: HIGH

Cooking time: 30 minutes

Utensil: trivet

2	eggplants
1 tbsp	(15 ml) olive oil
1	onion, finely chopped
1	garlic clove, smashed and chopped
2	tomatoes, cored and cut in wedges
5 tbsp	(75 ml) olive oil
5 tbsp	(75 ml) wine vinegar
	salt and pepper
	few drops lemon juice

Slice eggplants in half lengthwise. Score flesh deeply both crosswise and lengthwise; brush with 1 tbsp (15 ml) olive oil.

Place eggplant halves on trivet; microwave 30 minutes uncovered.

Scoop out cooked flesh and dice; place in mixing bowl.

Add remaining ingredients in order, toss well and serve.

Cheesy Cauliflower

(serves 4)

1 SERVING	171 CALORIES	8g CARBOHYDRATE
6g PROTEIN	13g FAT	1.1g FIBER

Setting: HIGH and MEDIUM-HIGH

Cooking time: 20 minutes

Utensil: 2-12 cups (3 L) casseroles

1	head cauliflower, washed and in flowerets
2 cups	(500 ml) hot water
¼ tsp	(1 ml) tarragon
¼ tsp	(1 ml) paprika
3 tbsp	(45 ml) butter
3 tbsp	(45 ml) flour
½ cup	(125 ml) grated cheddar cheese
	salt and pepper

Place cauliflower, water, tarragon and paprika in casserole. Season, cover and microwave 8 minutes at HIGH.

Stir flowerets slightly; replace cover and continue microwaving 6 minutes.

Using slotted spoon remove flowerets. Pour liquid into small bowl and replace cauliflower in casserole; set aside.

Place butter in second casserole. Microwave 2 minutes uncovered at HIGH.

Whisk in flour, then add reserved cauliflower liquid; mix well. Continue microwaving 2 minutes uncovered.

Whisk sauce well and correct seasoning. Pour over cauliflower and top with cheese; microwave 2 minutes uncovered at MEDIUM-HIGH.

1 Place celery, butter, ginger, chervil, salt and pepper in casserole. Cover and microwave 8 minutes.

3 Pour in chicken stock, mix and correct seasoning. Stir in tomato clam juice and microwave 10 minutes uncovered.

2 Add onion and flour; mix well.

4 Add apple sections and finish microwaving 4 minutes uncovered.

Braised Celery and Apple

(serves 4)

1 SERVING	100 CALORIES	16g CARBOHYDRATE
2g PROTEIN	3g FAT	1.0g FIBER

Setting: HIGH

Cooking time: 22 minutes

Utensil: 8 cups (2 L) casserole

4	large stalks celery, sliced thick
1 tbsp	(15 ml) butter
¼ tsp	(1 ml) ground ginger
½ tsp	(2 ml) chervil
1	onion, diced
3 tbsp	(45 ml) flour
1 cup	(250 ml) hot chicken stock
¼ cup	(50 ml) tomato clam juice
1	large apple, cored, peeled and cut into large sections
	salt and pepper

Place celery, butter, ginger, chervil, salt and pepper in casserole. Cover and microwave 8 minutes.

Add onion and flour; mix well.

Pour in chicken stock, mix and correct seasoning. Stir in tomato clam juice and microwave 10 minutes uncovered.

Add apple sections and finish microwaving 4 minutes uncovered.

Braised Yellow Squash

(serves 4)

1 SERVING	198 CALORIES	20g CARBOHYDRATE
5g PROTEIN	11g FAT	3.2g FIBER

Setting: HIGH and MEDIUM-HIGH

Cooking time: 11 minutes

Utensil: 12 cups (3 L) casserole

3 tbsp	(45 ml) butter
1	small onion, chopped
1	garlic clove, smashed and chopped
1¼ lb	(625 g) yellow squash
2	tomatoes, cored and cut in wedges
½ tsp	(2 ml) tarragon
½ cup	(125 ml) grated mozzarella cheese
	salt and pepper

Place butter, onion and garlic in casserole. Cover and microwave 3 minutes at HIGH.

Slice squash in half lengthwise and cut into pieces ½ in (1.2 cm) thick. Add to casserole with tomatoes; season with salt, pepper and tarragon. Microwave 3 minutes uncovered at HIGH.

Stir vegetables well; continue microwaving 3 minutes.

Sprinkle in cheese and finish microwaving 2 minutes uncovered at MEDIUM-HIGH.

Stuffed Peppers

(serves 2)

1 SERVING	610 CALORIES	59g CARBOHYDRATE
50g PROTEIN	19g FAT	6.3g FIBER

Setting: HIGH and MEDIUM
Cooking time: 10½ minutes
Utensil: 12 cups (3 L) casserole
8 cups (2 L) rectangular dish

2	large green peppers, cut into two and seeded
1 tbsp	(15 ml) oil
¼ lb	(125 g) lean ground beef
¼ lb	(125 g) lean ground veal
1	small onion, chopped
1	garlic clove, smashed and chopped
12 oz	(341 ml) can whole kernel corn, drained
2 tbsp	(30 ml) chili sauce
½ cup	(125 ml) grated mozzarella cheese
2 cups	(500 ml) hot tomato sauce
	salt and pepper

Place peppers in casserole with ½ cup (125 ml) salted, hot water. Cover and microwave 2 minutes at HIGH.

Remove peppers from casserole and set aside. Drain out water and dry casserole.

Place oil, both meats, onion and garlic in casserole; season well. Cover and microwave 2 minutes at HIGH.

Mix well and continue microwaving 30 seconds.

Stir in corn, chili sauce and cheese; season well. Cover and microwave 2 minutes at MEDIUM.

Stuff peppers with mixture and place in rectangular dish. Cover with tomato sauce and microwave 4 minutes covered at HIGH.

Hot Chick Pea Salad

(serves 4)

1 SERVING	300 CALORIES	28g CARBOHYDRATE
9g PROTEIN	17g FAT	5.5g FIBER

Setting: HIGH and MEDIUM-HIGH
Cooking time: 5 minutes
Utensil: 12 cups (3 L) casserole

1 tbsp	(15 ml) olive oil
1	small onion, finely diced
1	garlic clove, smashed and chopped
1	green pepper, finely diced
19 oz	(540 ml) can chick peas, drained and rinsed
¼ cup	(50 ml) olive oil
	juice 1½ lemons
	salt and freshly ground pepper

Place 1 tbsp (15 ml) oil, onion, garlic and green pepper in casserole. Cover and microwave 3 minutes at HIGH.

Stir in chick peas and season well; cover and microwave 2 minutes at MEDIUM-HIGH.

Transfer contents to large salad bowl. Pour in oil and lemon juice; toss, correct seasoning and serve hot or cold.

Poached Pears

(serves 3)

1 SERVING	157 CALORIES	39g CARBOHYDRATE
0g PROTEIN	0g FAT	4.8g FIBER

Setting: MEDIUM-HIGH

Cooking time: 7 minutes

Utensil:	8 cups (2 L) casserole
3	pears, cored and peeled
1 tbsp	(15 ml) rum
½ cup	(125 ml) hot water
¼ cup	(50 ml) brown sugar

Arrange pears in casserole with thick ends towards outside of dish.

Add remaining ingredients and microwave 4 minutes uncovered.

Rotate dish; continue microwaving 3 minutes.

Serve with chocolate sauce if desired.

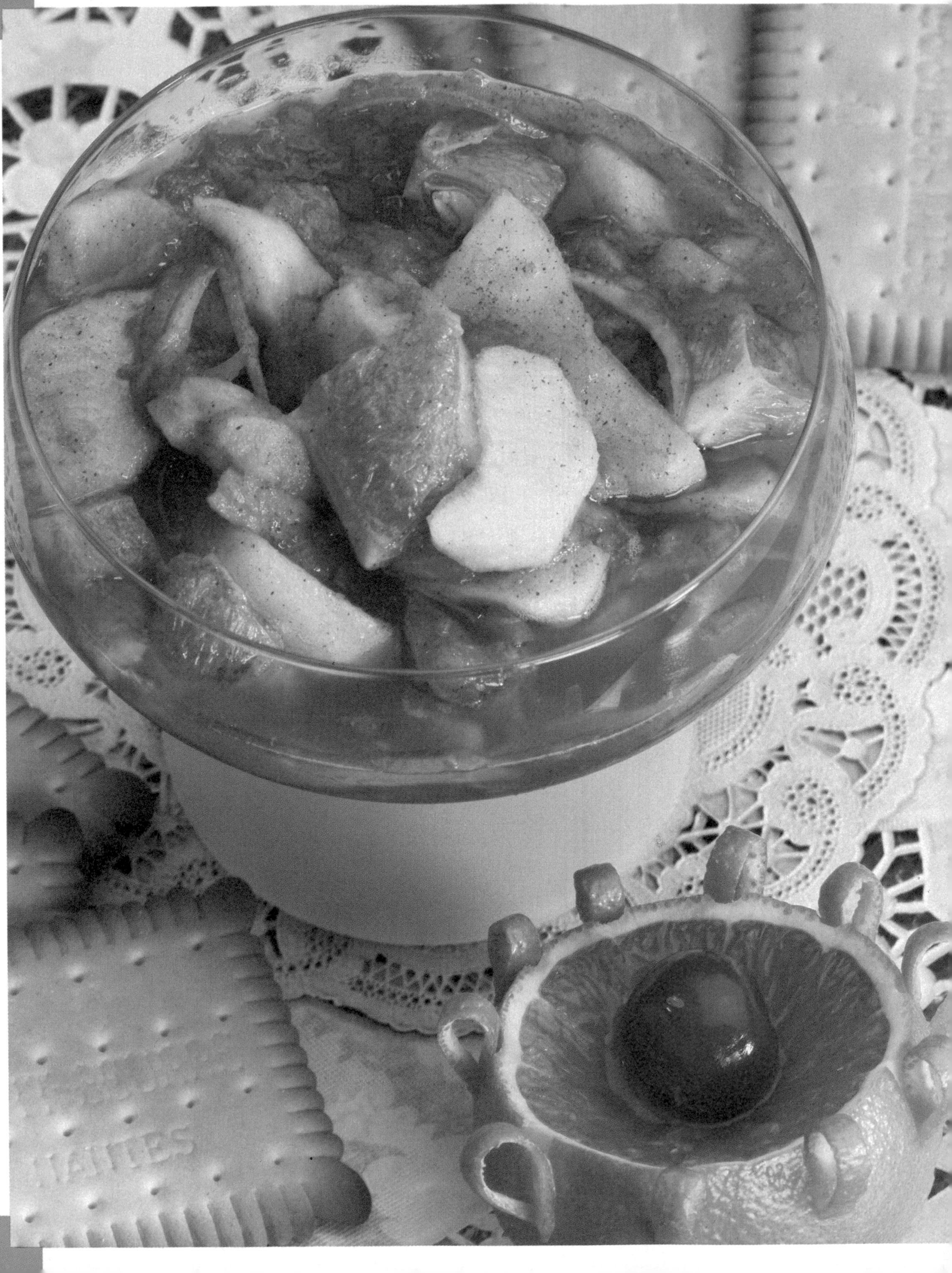

Crustless Fruit Cobbler

(serves 4)

1 SERVING	271 CALORIES	66g CARBOHYDRATE
1g PROTEIN	0g FAT	3.5g FIBER

Setting: HIGH

Cooking time: 8 minutes

Utensil: 12 cups (3 L) casserole

3	seedless oranges
4	sweet apples, cored, peeled and thinly sliced
½ cup	(125 ml) peach jelly
2 tbsp	(30 ml) brown sugar
¼ tsp	(1 ml) cinnamon
	rind of ¼ orange, thinly sliced and blanched

Use knife to peel oranges and remove white pith lining the rind. Dice oranges and place in casserole with apples.

Add peach jelly, brown sugar, cinnamon and thinly sliced blanched orange rind. Cover and microwave 4 minutes.

Mix well; replace cover and continue microwaving 4 minutes.

Remove casserole from microwave and let cool before serving.

Peach Melba

(serves 4)

1 SERVING	390 CALORIES	75g CARBOHYDRATE
4g PROTEIN	8g FAT	2.5g FIBER

Setting: HIGH

Cooking time: 7 minutes

Utensil: 8 cups (2 L) casserole

1½ cups	(375 ml) strawberries, hulled
¼ cup	(50 ml) currant jelly
½ cup	(125 ml) sugar
2 tbsp	(30 ml) orange liqueur
2 tbsp	(30 ml) cornstarch
4 tbsp	(60 ml) cold water
	grated rind of 1 lemon
	vanilla ice cream
	canned peach halves

Place strawberries, currant jelly, sugar, liqueur and lemon rind in casserole. Mix, cover and microwave 5 minutes.

Mix cornstarch with water; stir into strawberries and microwave 2 minutes uncovered.

Mix well and set aside to cool.

Serve fruit over ice cream and peach halves.

Quick Strawberry Topping

¼ cup (50 ml)	74 CALORIES	14g CARBOHYDRATE
0g PROTEIN	2g FAT	0.5g FIBER

Setting: HIGH
Cooking time: 7 minutes
Utensil: 12 cups (3 L) casserole

1½ cups	(375 ml) frozen strawberries
½ cup	(125 ml) sugar
2 tbsp	(30 ml) butter
2 tbsp	(30 ml) orange liqueur
2 tbsp	(30 ml) cornstarch
4 tbsp	(60 ml) cold water

Place strawberries, sugar, butter and liqueur in casserole. Cover and microwave 5 minutes.

Mix strawberries well. Mix cornstarch with water; stir into fruit. Microwave 2 minutes uncovered.

Cool, then purée in food processor. Serve over ice cream, cake or pudding.

Raspberry and Kiwi Parfait

(serves 4)

1 SERVING	307 CALORIES	48g CARBOHYDRATE
4g PROTEIN	11g FAT	4.2g FIBER

Setting: HIGH
Cooking time: 7 minutes
Utensil: 12 cups (3 L) casserole

1	small envelope unflavored gelatine
¼ cup	(50 ml) cold water
2 cups	(500 ml) raspberries
4	kiwis, peeled and diced
½ cup	(125 ml) sugar
1 tsp	(5 ml) vanilla
3	egg whites, beaten stiff
½ cup	(125 ml) heavy cream, whipped

Sprinkle gelatine over water poured into bowl, do not mix and set aside.

Place raspberries and kiwis in casserole. Add sugar, vanilla and mix well. Cover and microwave 4 minutes.

Mix well; cover and continue microwaving 2 minutes.

Stir in gelatine and microwave 1 minute uncovered.

Cool, then purée in food processor.

Transfer puréed fruit to bowl and fold in beaten egg whites and whipped cream. Serve chilled in tall dessert glasses.

Homemade Fruit Sundae

(serves 4)

1 SERVING	112 CALORIES	22g CARBOHYDRATE
1g PROTEIN	2g FAT	2.4g FIBER

Setting: MEDIUM-HIGH and HIGH
Cooking time: 5 minutes
Utensil: 8 cups (2 L) casserole

2 cups	(500 ml) strawberries, hulled
2 tbsp	(30 ml) finely grated lemon rind
2-3 tbsp	(30-45 ml) sugar
1 tbsp	(15 ml) cornstarch
2 tbsp	(30 ml) cold water
½ cup	(125 ml) raspberries
	juice 1 orange

Place strawberries, lemon rind, sugar and orange juice in casserole. Cover and microwave 3 minutes at MEDIUM-HIGH.

Mix cornstarch with water; stir into strawberries. Add raspberries and microwave 2 minutes uncovered at HIGH.

Cool before serving over ice cream. Decorate with candies or serve with cookies if desired.

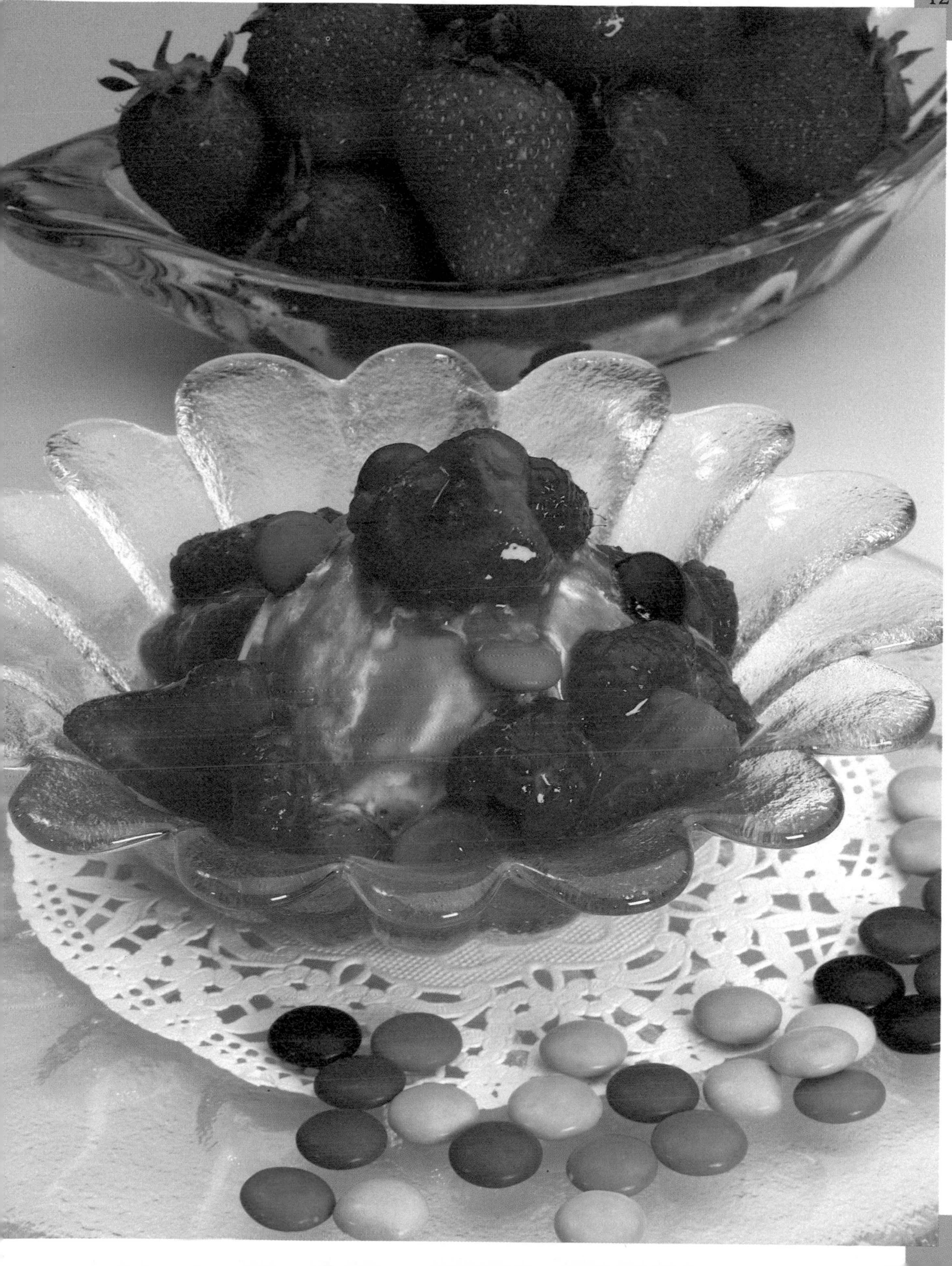

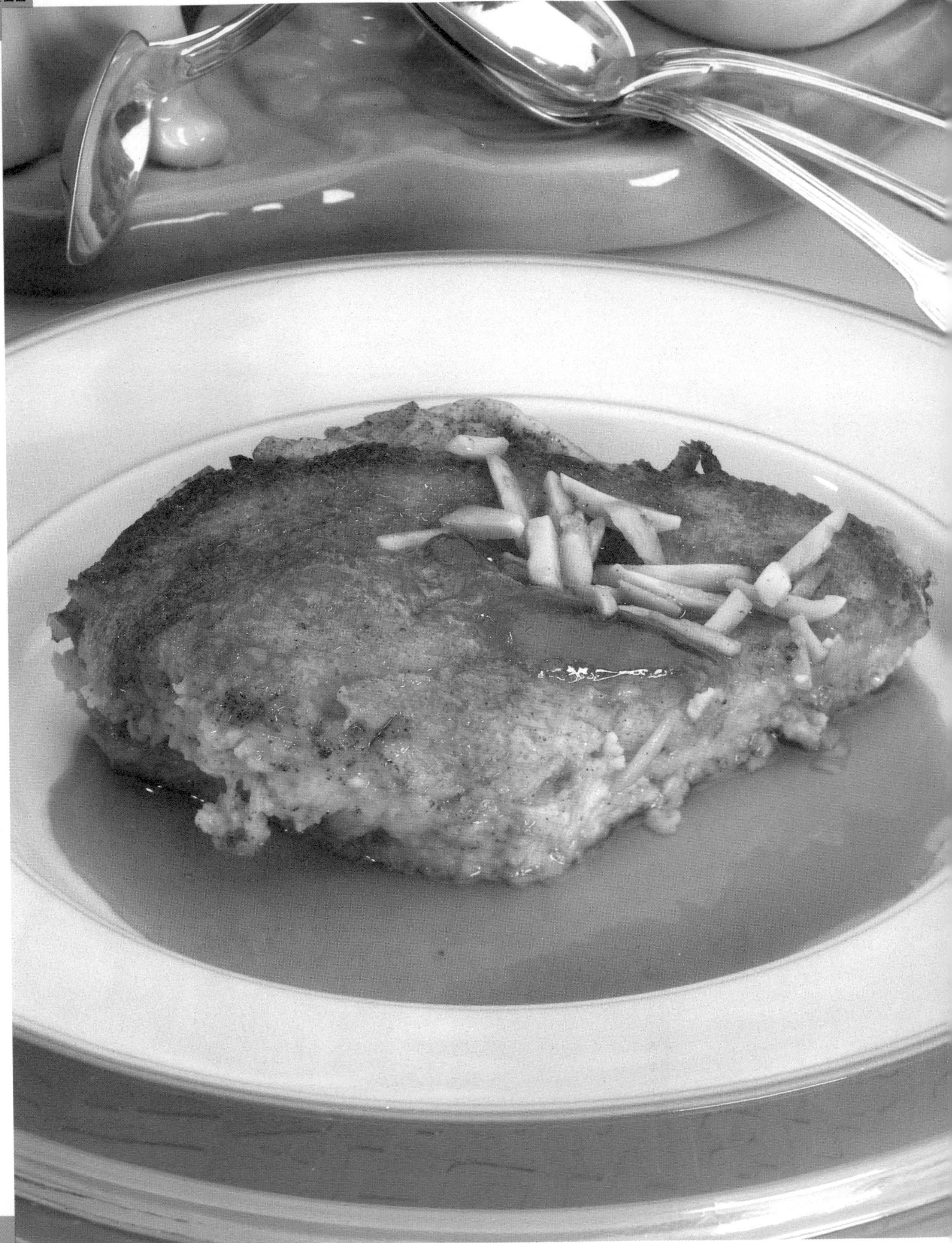

Wholesome Bread Pudding

(serves 6 to 8)

1 SERVING	226 CALORIES	39g CARBOHYDRATE
8g PROTEIN	4g FAT	1.3g FIBER

Setting: MEDIUM-HIGH

Cooking time: 12 minutes

Utensil: 6 cups (1.5 L) square dish

4	large, thick slices day-old bread, toasted
½ cup	(125 ml) strawberry jam or jelly
¼ cup	(50 ml) slivered almonds
1½ tbsp	(25 ml) butter
4	eggs
¼ cup	(50 ml) sugar
3 tbsp	(45 ml) flour
1 tbsp	(15 ml) cinnamon
1½ cups	(375 ml) milk

Arrange bread to fit in buttered dish, trimming slices if needed.

Spread jam over bread, sprinkle on almonds and dot with butter; set aside.

Place eggs in bowl and beat with electric hand mixer. Beat in sugar.

Add flour and cinnamon; beat well. Pour in milk and beat until combined.

Pour mixture over bread in dish. Microwave 12 minutes uncovered.

Serve plain or if desired with syrup.

Arrange bread **1** fit in buttered dish, trimming slices if needed.

3 Sprinkle on almonds and dot with butter.

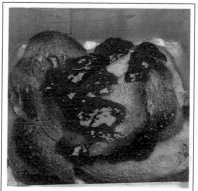

Spread jam **2** over bread.

4 Pour milk mixture over bread and microwave 12 minutes uncovered.

Banana Luncheon Cake

(serves 6 to 8)

1 SERVING	303 CALORIES	36g CARBOHYDRATE
4g PROTEIN	16g FAT	0.6g FIBER

Setting: MEDIUM-HIGH
Cooking time: 15 minutes
Utensil: bundt mold

2	bananas, sliced
4 tbsp	(60 ml) rum
¾ cup	(175 ml) sugar
1½ tbsp	(25 ml) cinnamon
½ cup	(125 ml) vegetable oil
2	eggs
1 cup	(250 ml) all-purpose flour
2 tsp	(10 ml) baking powder
¼ tsp	(1 ml) salt
¼ tsp	(1 ml) baking soda
¼ cup	(50 ml) milk
1 tbsp	(15 ml) vanilla

Place bananas in food processor and blend 1 minute. Add rum and continue blending 30 seconds. Set aside.

Place sugar, cinnamon and oil in bowl; beat with electric hand mixer until combined.

Add eggs and continue beating about 2 minutes.

Fold in bananas, mixing well with spatula; set aside.

Mix dry ingredients together and whisk into banana mixture.

Pour in milk and vanilla; mix again until smooth.

Pour batter into oiled bundt mold and microwave 5 minutes uncovered.

Rotate mold; continue microwaving 5 minutes.

Rotate mold again; finish microwaving 5 minutes.

Remove mold from microwave and let cake stand 10 minutes before unmolding.

Slice and serve with a frosting of icing sugar for a special treat.

Place bananas in food processor and blend 1 minute. Add rum and continue blending 30 seconds; set aside.

Place sugar, cinnamon and oil in bowl; beat with electric hand mixer until combined.

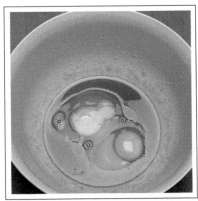

Add eggs and continue beating about 2 minutes.

Fold in bananas then mix well with spatula.

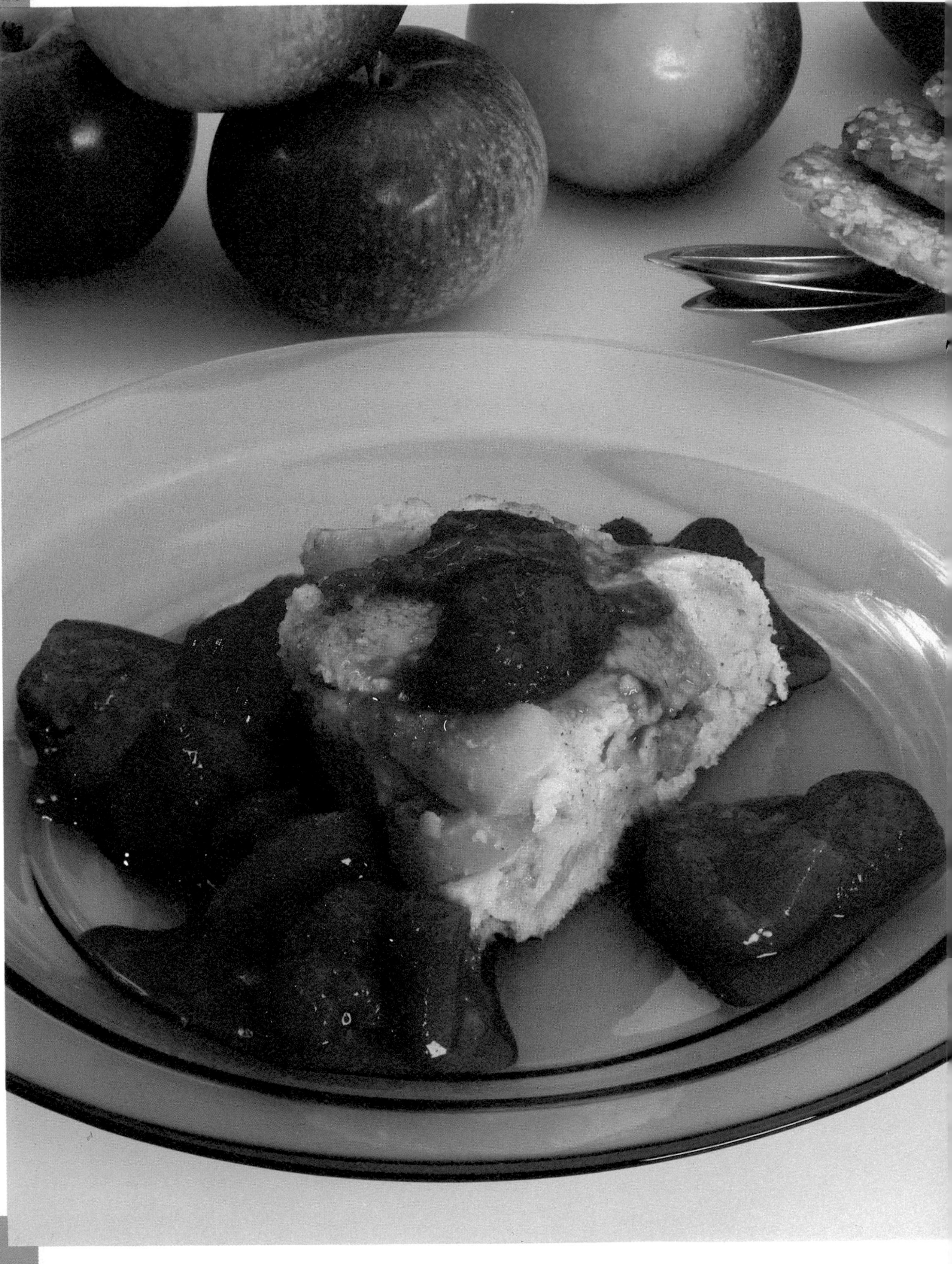

Apple Rum Cake

(serves 6 to 8)

SERVING	288 CALORIES	31g CARBOHYDRATE
5g PROTEIN	17g FAT	1.0g FIBER

Setting: MEDIUM-HIGH

Cooking time: 15 minutes

Utensil: 8 cups (2 L) round dish

	cooking apples, cored, peeled and sliced
2 tbsp	(30 ml) rum
2 tbsp	(30 ml) cinnamon
½ cup	(125 ml) oil
½ cup	(125 ml) sugar
	eggs

½ cup	(125 ml) all-purpose flour
1 tsp	(5 ml) baking powder
	pinch salt

Toss apples, rum and cinnamon together in bowl; set aside.

Place oil and sugar in another bowl. Add eggs and beat until frothy.

Mix dry ingredients together and fold into egg mixture; beat until well incorporated.

Stir in apples and pour batter into buttered dish. Microwave 5 minutes uncovered.

Rotate dish; continue microwaving 5 minutes.

Rotate dish again; finish microwaving 5 minutes.

Remove dish from microwave and let cake stand 10 minutes before unmolding.

Serve with strawberry sauce if desired or with vanilla ice cream.

Toss apples, rum and cinnamon together in bowl; set aside.

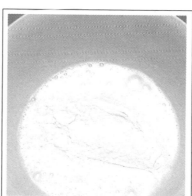 **3** Fold dry ingredients into egg mixture; beat until well incorporated.

Place oil and sugar in another bowl. Add eggs and beat until frothy.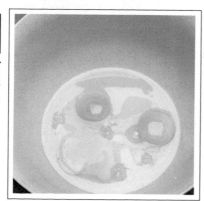

 Stir in apples.

Double Cheesecake

(serves 6 to 8)

1 SERVING	483 CALORIES	43g CARBOHYDRATE
6g PROTEIN	26g FAT	0.3g FIBER

Setting: HIGH and MEDIUM-HIGH

Cooking time: 12 minutes 45 seconds

Utensil: 6 cups (1.5 L) glass pie plate

1½ cups	(375 ml) Graham cracker crumbs
1 cup	(250 ml) sugar
⅓ cup	(75 ml) soft butter
8 oz	(250 g) cream cheese, room temperature
4 oz	(125 g) cottage cheese
½ cup	(125 ml) heavy cream
2 tbsp	(30 ml) grated orange rind
3	eggs
1 tsp	(5 ml) vanilla

Combine cracker crumbs, half of sugar and butter together with pastry cutter. Press into pie plate and microwave 1¾ minutes uncovered at HIGH. Remove and set aside to cool.

Place both cheeses in mixing bowl. Add heavy cream, remaining sugar and orange rind; beat together with electric hand mixer until smooth.

Beat in vanilla.

Add eggs, one at a time, beating well between additions.

Pour batter into pie crust and microwave 7 minutes uncovered at MEDIUM-HIGH.

Rotate plate; continue microwaving 4 minutes.

Remove from microwave and set aside to cool.

Slice and serve with fruit topping if desired.

Fresh Raspberries with Custard Cream

(serves 4)

1 SERVING	407 CALORIES	57g CARBOHYDRATE
11g PROTEIN	15g FAT	3.8g FIBER

Setting: HIGH

Cooking time: 2 minutes 30 seconds

Utensil: 8 cups (2 L) casserole

2 cups	(500 ml) fresh raspberries
2 tbsp	(30 ml) brandy
2	kiwis, peeled and diced large
3 tbsp	(45 ml) brown sugar
1 tsp	(5 ml) cornstarch
½ cup	(125 ml) granulated sugar
2	whole eggs
3	egg yolks
1 tbsp	(15 ml) vanilla
2 cups	(500 ml) hot milk
½ cup	(125 ml) hot light cream

Place raspberries, brandy, kiwis and brown sugar in bowl; toss and marinate 1 hour at room temperature.

Meanwhile, place cornstarch and granulated sugar in casserole. Add all eggs and whisk well.

Add vanilla, hot milk and cream; mix very well with whisk. Microwave 1½ minutes uncovered.

Whisk and continue microwaving 1 minute.

Cool and serve sauce with marinated fruit.

Coconut Custard

(serves 4)

1 SERVING	245 CALORIES	22g CARBOHYDRATE
10g PROTEIN	13g FAT	0.3g FIBER

Setting: MEDIUM

Cooking time: 11 minutes

Utensil: individual custard dishes

4	beaten eggs
¼ cup	(50 ml) sugar
1 tsp	(5 ml) vanilla
½ cup	(125 ml) shredded coconut
1 tbsp	(15 ml) cornstarch
3 tbsp	(45 ml) cold water
2 cups	(500 ml) hot milk

Mix beaten eggs with sugar until well blended.

Add vanilla and coconut; whisk well.

Mix cornstarch with water; stir into batter. Pour in milk and incorporate well.

Pour into custard dishes and place in microwave. Microwave 5 minutes uncovered.

Rotate dishes and continue microwaving 6 minutes. The custard is cooked when firm.

Cool at room temperature, then chill before serving.